The House

the Cradle of Destiny

Hugh Rayment

Order this book online at www.trafford.com
or email orders@trafford.com

Most Trafford titles are also available at major online book retailers.

Printed in Victoria, BC, Canada.

ISBN: 978-1-4269-1578-9

*Our mission is to efficiently provide the world's finest, most comprehensive
book publishing service, enabling every author to experience success.
To find out how to publish your book, your way, and have it available
worldwide, visit us online at www.trafford.com/10510*

Trafford rev. 2/9/2010

 www.trafford.com

North America & international
toll-free: 1 888 232 4444 (USA & Canada)
phone: 250 383 6864 ◆ fax: 812 355 4082

Acknowledgments

To my brother Tom for his flattering and his witty remarks and for remembering those days and events so many years ago. To the rest of my siblings for jogging my memory of days gone by. In the many family reunions over the years many a story has been told about our time of growing up in that wonderful old house on the farm so that it has remained clear as a bell in my mind over the years.

I extend a very sincere thank you to my wife, Elsie, for putting up with the many hours I spent in the computer room while preparing the manuscript for the publisher. I also thank all those who supported and encouraged me during the two years it took to complete. To my daughter, Judy for proofreading my script and tabulating typos and making corrections for the final editing and printing by Trafford Publishing of Victoria, B.C.

I thank all of you.   Hugh

Forward

Storytellers have always held a special place in human society. They keep us in touch with who we are and where we come from. Occasionally we are fortunate enough to find a storyteller who will take the time and trouble to share his story with us and write it down. Our author is just such a skilled storyteller who writes, not only from personal memory, but from careful research as well as from his interest in fiction.

In fact what I remember most about my brother, when I was a child, was his ability to invent stories to amuse and sometimes scare his younger siblings. Little did we know that this skill would bear fruit many years later when Hugh became a serious writer.

Let me assure you that this book is not a work of fiction, because I also experienced or witnessed much of the early years of Hugh's story. Even after he left home we always kept in touch throughout his war experiences and his varied and eventful careers since then. In fact we both ended up working for the same employer, Edmonton Public Schools; I as a school counselor and work experience coordinator, and he as a competent vocational teacher. Both retired now, we have time to reflect on the past and he has asked me to write this forward for him.

Rev. Cannon Tom Rayment

Introduction

On my dining room wall hangs a large picture of a dilapidated old farmhouse. There is no glass in the windows, part of the kitchen has fallen away, and its boards are frowning with age. It seems to be crying out for a story to be told about its history and that of the people who lived there. This is the house where I grew up with my brothers and sisters, and stands as a monument to a pioneer family in north central Alberta. I doubt if it will finally crumble to the ground until all of us have gone to our maker. That is where my mother and father came on their honeymoon and remained there for some twenty years following WW1.

I have accepted the challenge of writing this book in memory of all those people who influenced my life during the formative years of my childhood on the farm and my adult life up until the present time. Especially I dedicate this book to my family and particularly to my wife, Elsie, who joined me 60 years ago and has shared in our many adventures and career changes ever since. I write with hopes that readers will get some enjoyment from it and perhaps some inspiration as well. I have spent almost three years researching and editing this book and have tried to express my opinions of the events that have influenced my life over the past 85 years. I also reflect upon some of my observations of the conditions that prevail in our society up to the present time, with particular emphasis on the family

Chapter One**

Albert Hugh Rayment was born in London, England on December fourth, 1888 to a middle class family. The Rayment home was located in the fashionable district of Child's Hill and still stands to this day. They lived in comfortable circumstances and, as was the custom in this class, Albert was sent off to a boys' boarding school at a very young age. Being a faithful Anglican family the school chosen was St. Paul's in London. Albert was enrolled in the famous St. Paul's Boy's Choir where he received the finest of voice training. He sang regularly with St. Paul's Choir in St. Paul's Cathedral as well as many other places in London. He sang at the coronation of Edward the seventh at Westminster Abby. As a point of interest the coronation was postponed for a week because the Prince suffered a case of appendicitis. Albert remained as a choirboy until his voice broke at about age thirteen. Albert's interest in music, and particularly singing, lasted throughout his life.

Little is known of Albert's school life other than his mention of his favorite sports of cricked, tennis, and rugby. The headmaster ruled, handling discipline by the use of the cane. A boy who stepped out of line was ordered to fetch the cane and bring it to the headmaster who applied the necessary strokes to fit the crime. Albert, though generally a well behaved lad, did occasionally get sent for the cane. Under the British school system, the student's route through school was decided at a very young age. Basic education included reading, writing, arithmetic, as well as Latin, French, and in some cases Greek. Albert took all of these subjects. At age thirteen the split took place according to what course the student wanted to pursue. Albert wanted to be an architect so he chose that line of study and was enrolled at Merchant Taylor's Technical School.

Upon graduation, Albert started his apprenticeship. It was the custom that the apprentice take up residence with the journeyman who immersed him in intensive training as well as controlling his home and social behavior, i.e. the apprentice must attend Church every Sunday. The first year the parents paid the journeyman for training their son. As the lad became more productive the rate decreased and in the final year he may receive a small remuneration for his work. Albert was successful and was employed by the firm where he took his training. About a year after graduation Albert attended a banquet and became suddenly ill. Perhaps he had eaten the wrong part of a crab or something. The doctors recommended that he live in a dryer climate. His parents suggested Australia so away he went, working his way on a cattle boat. His health didn't seem to improve and he couldn't stand the heat so after two years he returned to London. The doctors suggested that he move out of the London fog; perhaps to the midlands. So Albert was off again and found work on a dairy farm near Nottingham.

At this time; about 1910, there was a lot of advertising directing young men to the Colonies and in particular to Canada. In 1911 Albert boarded a ship to Halifax where he boarded a train to Alberta. Homesteads were available and

Albert obtained a quarter section east of Edmonton in the Viking district. When he got off the train the real estate sharks were there to offer great deals for lots in a little whistle stop place by the name of Poe.

They had elaborate plans showing street car lines and a boom town. Today there is nothing there but a gas station.

Albert and two other "green Englishmen" got together and pooled their expertise to build modest shacks on their properties. The deal was that they had to fence their land and break a few acres for seeding grain. They were also to take up residence on the land for 10 months in the first year in order to prove up their homesteads. There was the threat that an inspector could come out to see that they were following the rules. Albert spent his first winter in a tent in spite of the begging of a nearby established pioneer to bunk in with him in a house. Albert banked the tent up with straw and snow and said that it wasn't too bad even though the temperature went below -50 degrees F. For a heater he used a five gallon oil drum which also served as a stove. He survived the winter with few mishaps but in the spring, while he was out hunting jack rabbits for food, one of his cows walked into his tent and pulled it down. Spring also brought swarms of mosquitoes but Albert's pioneer spirit held fast and he got on with creating his farm. These men worked from sun-up to sun-down and got their shacks up before the next winter storms.

As time went on they were able to take vegetables from their gardens and diets improved greatly. In the second year they were able to harvest a modest amount of grain from the newly ploughed fertile land. At least they had a few dollars to buy staples for the table. Letters home indicated that all was well on the homestead. The life of a bachelor was quite lonely and there was very little social activity but the hard work kept them busy. A new school was built nearby and Albert was briefly attracted by the young lady that taught there. This did not last because World War 1 was in its second year. Many of the homesteaders were from England and felt loyal to the old country and enlisted in the Army. Albert was among them and wet to Edmonton and joined the Army at the Prince of Wales Armoury. WW1 was a ghastly conflict with thousands of lives lost in trench warfare. The battle lines stretched across Europe, in some places the opposing trenches were only thirty yards apart. The troops lived in rat infested trenches that often held a foot of muddy water. Lice infested their clothes and made life misery; at times worse than the bullets and shells. Albert fought the Germans in such famed places as Mons Yepres, Pashendale, and Vimy Ridge. The war ended for him when he was wounded at Vimy. He was hospitalized in England until he regained his strength and by this time the war was over.

During this period of healing Albert was able to connect with family members and his cousin Helen Elizabeth Yeatman was a frequent visitor to his bedside. They had been infatuated with one another as children and now they were into some serious courting. Of course it caused some furor with the parents because of the relationship. Albert had to report back to duty for return to Canada and discharge so a decision had to be made. It was decided that Albert would return to Canada and get the farm going and then Helen would join him and they would get married. With a tearful farewell at Southampton Albert once more boarded a ship for Canada.

Albert arrived in Halifax after six days of rough seas and sea sickness. The ship was crowded with veterans and new settlers and what personal belongings they could bring with them. There were crates of furniture; much of it of high quality. Some brought their pianos and most of them had large trunks full of clothing and personal belongings. Most of the men wore top hats and all the women wore stylish hats, long dresses, and button shoes. They would be an odd looking assortment if seen today but of course that was the style of the day. Those passengers not remaining in Halifax, boarded trains heading west.

The long journey had just begun. The first landmark after leaving Halifax was a deep gorge cut for the railway bed. It had been cut out by manual labor, mostly Chinese immigrants who worked with picks and shovels for 25 cents a day. The train passed through the beautiful Maritimes and on to the province of Quebec. The first major stop was at Montreal where they could get off and stretch their legs. Some of them crossed the street to the shops to get some treats and this is where they discovered that the people spoke French. On board again they traveled into Ontario and along the north shore of the Great Lakes. The distance was incredible, especially for those from Britain where no trip took more than a day. It took three days and two nights of steady travel to cross this province. They saw nothing but trees and rock and hundreds of lakes. Finally they crossed into Manitoba. The newcomers that got off in Winnipeg got their first taste of a prairie winter with the temperature sitting at -40F. A good number of settlers disembarked in Winnipeg to seek homesteads with hopes of a prosperous new life. The journey for Albert finally ended in Edmonton, arriving in early March. It had taken fourteen days of steady travel and now it was his turn to look for land. While in Edmonton Albert went to see the Soldiers' Board. Under a special deal for veterans he could get land at a very reasonable price and funds to buy machinery and some stock to get him started. He still had the original homestead but it was only a quarter section and he wanted a half section so he settled for land three miles from the homestead. A farmer by the name of Walty owned the half section and it was for sale. Albert got the land through the Soldiers' Settlement Board and was particularly pleased to find that there was a house and barn on the property. It would not be practical to try and farm both properties so he sold the homestead and, with the help of some neighbors, moved his shack to the new place where it served as a work shop for many years to come.

The new farm was located in a district named Rodino. The next door neighbor, by the name of Robert MacFarlane was the Postmaster for the district. He went to Minburn, a town fourteen miles away, and picked up the mail. Residents could call at his place to get their mail, buy stamps, and mail letters. It took two to three weeks to get mail from the Old Country and visa versa. Rodino School was built on four acres of Albert's land. It was a one roomer and accommodated up to twenty students from grade one to grade nine.

Albert got calling cards sent from England that read as follows;

Albert Hugh Rayment Esq.
Summersdale Farm
Rodino, Alberta
Canada.

There was no postal code; as a matter of fact there was no telephone, no electricity, and no radio let alone running water or natural gas. Coal oil lamps provided light and heat was gained from wood stoves and heaters. Coal was available when it could be afforded. Albert was kept very busy running the farm and making improvements to the house for his bride.

He looked forward to Helen's letters. She wrote every day and he received bunches of them every Saturday. He also kept her in touch with everything he did on the farm so that she would have some idea what it would be like to live on a farm.

About this time, 1920, there was a terrible influenza epidemic and many perished from the dread disease. In spite of the fact that the closest doctor was eighteen miles away, Albert managed to survive with no noticeable side effects. A neighbor, Tommy Daniel, another veteran had been wounded in the war and as he recovered in England he fell in love with his nurse. They were married in England and joined the rush to find land in the new world. They settled in the Rodino district at the same time as Albert. Mrs. Tommy [Vi] was the only person with medical experience and she saved many lives during that epidemic. She accepted no remuneration and walked many miles to help the ill. She walked the two miles through snow drifts to nurse Albert and even fed and watered his livestock. Many owed their lives to her. Neighbors who were not stricken pitched in and helped those with the flu. This is how they survived.

Albert recovered from the flu in time to get his crop seeded and put in a vegetable garden. He had a good crop of wheat that year because the soil was rich and there was enough rain to insure good growth. He got a good crop of potatoes and other vegetables so things were looking pretty rosy. During the summer Albert broke more land with a new McKormick Deering breaking plow. It had a single large breaking shear with a depth lever and two handles behind. The operator guided the plow by the handles and drove the four horses required to pull the machine. He had to walk behind with one foot in the furrow and the other on the overturned sod. It was backbreaking work that had to be done. In the early days Albert plowed around bushes and sloughs to save time and would tackle that later on. In the long, hot summer days Albert worked at getting hay in the yard for winter. There was plenty of upland grass and slough grass. First the grass had to be cut with a mower and then, when it was dry, raked into piles, and then hauled to the yard on a hay rack. Albert had learned the art of stacking hay when he worked at the dairy-farm in England. It had to be done right so that no moisture got into the stack as this would spoil the hay making it use-less as feed for the stock. Farmers took great pride in plowing a straight line and building fine looking hay stacks. In the meantime the cows had to be milked, fed and watered so it can be seen that farming was no easy task.

In the meantime the crop was ripening and Albert had to prepare for the harvest. If it rained the harvest would have to stop. On these days Albert busied himself with building a fence for a new pasture. This operation required posts cut from willow trees in five foot lengths. They had to be sharp-ened on one end and the distributed along the fence line at ten foot intervals. The next step was to dig holes for the posts and then pound them into the ground with a heavy post maul. They had to be in a perfect straight line and then three stands of barbed wire stapled to the posts about sixteen inches be-tween strands. All of Albert's fences were dead straight and a job he was proud of.

Now it was time for the harvest. As soon as the grain was ready Albert hooked four horses to the binder and cut grain from sun-up to sun-dawn. The binder tied the grain into sheaves with binder twine and then the operator shifted the bundle carrier to deposit the bundles in groups six and in rows. The next job was putting the bundles up into stooks to shed off rain. Now all was ready for the threshing crew to come in and complete the harvest. The bundles were picked up in horse drawn bundle racks and hauled to the threshing machine. The bundles were fed into the feeder and the grain was separated from the straw and chaff. The straw went out the blower into a large straw pile. The grain came out of the grain pipe into a wagon and was hauled to the granary located in the farm yard. It was stored there until convenient to haul to the elevator for sale. Here the farmer was issued a grain check based on amount and quality of the grain.

Typically the threshing crew was made up of local farmers and their wages were deducted to pay their own threshing bill which was based upon so much per bushel threshed. Usually there was a bunk house that went along with the crew and many a good story was told there in the evening after a hard days work. The women seemed to compete to see who could cook up the best meals for the crew. The day would start before sun-up and go till it was too dark to work. The first chore was to feed the horses and harness them ready for another day in the field. Next was a hearty breakfast and then off to work. There was a tea break half way through the morning and again in mid afternoon. The mid-day meal and dinner were feasts fit for a king. Yes, threshing time was a time for great excitement and even the teacher allowed the kids to watch a threshing crew pass the school.

Albert and Helen had decided that they would get married before Christmas as soon as she arrived from England. The nearest place Albert could get an Anglican minister and as hotel room was in Vermillion, about forty miles from the farm. The 5th of December, 1920 Albert hitched up the team to the sleigh and set out to meet his bride. The temperature that day stood at -40 F but there was no wind. He had filled the sleigh box with hay and plenty of blankets to make a cozy nest. He got his horses into the livery stable, secured a hotel room and met with Rev. H.A. Edwards to make final arrangements for the wedding in St. Saviors Church. The following day Albert was at the station in plenty of time to see Helen step from the train. She climbed into the sleigh for her first sleigh ride ever. It was a small but intimate wedding and they spent their honeymoon night in the Vermillion Hotel.

The next morning they had to make an early start for the long trip to the farm. Albert had got the hotel staff to heat up a large rock to place in the sleight to fend off a bit of the cold. The trip took all of six hours before they finally turned in the gate to home. Here Helen learned one very necessary lesson about farm life. The horses had to be put in the barn and fed and the other animals looked after before even going to the house. When they entered the house it was cold. A neighbor had come in and banked up the heater with coal but it had died down. Albert got the kitchen stove going and produced a pot of frozen stew to put on the stove. They were young and in love and Helen took it in her stride as an exciting adventure.

The happy couple was just finishing supper when they heard a huge

din outside. It was the neighbors who had come to welcome the new bride with a chivaree. They were banging pots and pans and shouting their greetings. They brought wedding gifts for the bride and they brought plenty of something else. It was moonshine and other homemade concoctions. One of the guests had a violin to make music. Soon the party was rolling and although Helen was a bit bewildered, she did join in, but only for a couple of hours. She and Albert went upstairs to bed.

Albert woke up early and got the fires going and made Helen a cup of tea. When she came out of the bedroom a sorry sight met her eyes. There were empty bottles lying around on the floor and the place was a mess. To add to it there was a man passed out in a wash tub. Although it was never mentioned I imagine there were a few tears shed that day. All these neighbors soon became good friends of the Rayments who later took part in similar parties themselves. It was part of country living.

In the first few weeks Helen gradually became accustomed to the cold but the lack of electricity and running water was almost unbearable. When she wanted a bath Albert had to bring snow in from outside and melt it on the stove. And when the water was hot it was poured into a big round wash tub placed by the heater. The water was nice and soft but Helen was without the privacy of a bathroom. There were no curtains on the windows at this time but then the windows were coated with a thick layer of frost until the warm weather came. The toilet consisted of a two-hole job about 100 yards from the house. Albert had purchased a pot at an auction sale and it was placed under the bed and emptied each morning. If forgotten it would freeze solid and would have to be thawed with hot water to empty it. This sort of refuse was dumped into a pit a distance from the house.

The drinking water was pumped from a hand-dug well but it was very hard. Water pails were red with rust but the water tasted alright. It was good for watering the stock and there was a good supply of it. In the spring water was hauled from a slough and had to be strained through a cloth to remove water creatures and other debris. This water was used for washing clothes which was done by hand in a wash tub. There was no laundry soap as we know it today. Housewives had to learn to make lye soap. It consisted of beef fat mixed with lye. It was allowed to set in a box and then cut into bars. It made good laundry soap but when Helen wrote home to England she often asked them to send her some bars of proper toilet soap. Wash day was Monday and Helen slaved away with a scrub board to get the grime out of Albert's work clothes. The clothes were hung out to dry on the page wire fence. In the winter they froze and had to be pried off and placed by the stove to thaw before they could be ironed with a flat iron heated on the stove. Women took great pride in hanging out a white wash. Everything was ironed and patched as necessary. Sometimes there were patches on top of patches because money was scarce and new clothes could not always be bought.

There were no cement walks so mud got tracked into the house and the kitchen floor had to be scrubbed at least once a week. The dog tracked in mud and on the odd occasion a chicken would wander into the house if the door were left open. It was necessary to have at least two or three cats on the farm to control the mice. Most farms had several barn cats to keep the mice down in the grain stacks.

The cows had to be milked morning and night regardless of anything else. They were milked by hand into pails and then the milk was carried to the house, strained into the separator which separated the cream into a cream pail. The cream was saved in 5 or 8 gallon cream cans to be sold to the creamery once a week. This provided enough money to buy such things a sugar and other condiments for the kitchen. Enough cream was kept out to make butter for family use. The excess milk was fed to the calves and the pigs. Plenty of whole milk was saved for drinking and cooking.

Chapter Two

With a good deal of help from other pioneer ladies, Helen became accustomed to farm life and was soon helping other new arrivals to adjust. After about three months Helen announced to Albert that she was pregnant and the baby would be born in November when there was a good chance of snow and cold weather. A new hospital had been built in Viking, about eighteen miles from the farm. Albert was delighted of course about the baby but had some terrible thoughts of how he would get Helen to the hospital, especially if they got an early snowfall. Nevertheless Albert put his mind to farming. He had a good crop that year and had a few extra dollars to spend. He went to an auction and bought a democrat. It had leaf springs and an upholstered seat and an open luggage compartment in the back. Some of these vehicles were closed in but this one was open to the elements. With good warm clothing and a couple of blankets it was quite comfortable; much more than the wagon. It was put to good use and made travel much more comfortable. When it was very cold out Albert would heat up a rock in the oven and place it in a bed of straw in the front of the seat. However it was not a good vehicle to travel in the snow. When the snow came all was transferred to the sleigh. As when Helen first arrived, the sleigh could be made quite comfortable as well. At least the passengers could snuggle down in the straw and be out of the wind. In very cold weather the sleigh runners squealed as they passed over ice and snow.

Helen had a relatively easy pregnancy despite the hot summer and the hard work. She managed to get the help of a neighboring girl, Effie Faulkner. She looked after the house cleaning, milking and was joy to have around. Actually she stayed on after the baby came, attending school and working for Helen after school.

Toward the end of October Albert kept an eye on the weather. If it snowed they would have to go in the sleigh but if not they could use the democrat. At last Helen started to have labor pains. Albert wasted no time bringing the democrat around and getting Helen seated as comfortable as possible. In a mad dash they were off over frozen and rutty roads to Viking. They made it in record time and Helen was admitted to hospital. Ten hours later Helen gave birth to a healthy baby boy. She was confined to bed for a week, which was the custom then. They named the baby Albert Fredrick, later to go by the name of Fred. There was a heavy snowfall that week so Albert had to take the sleigh. The weather was quite mild for the trip to the farm and they took a leisurely trip home.

Despite the cold weather they were able to keep the house warm enough. Albert was able to afford a load of coal. He hauled it from the mine at Riley which was 40 miles away. The coal would keep the fire going all night without having to get up and stoke. With the new baby came extra work such as washing diapers and baby clothes. Helen was able to breast feed little Freddy so there was not much to do with baby bottles. With Effie's help they got through the winter in fine style.

The following July Helen once more announced that she was pregnant. Once again there were adjustments to be made. Fred's iron cot could still fit in the bedroom and the new baby could be placed in a wicker basket on a table near the bed. Upon the arrival of a new baby the older ones could graduate to the big bedroom upstairs. It was very cold up there but with plenty of blankets it had to do. There was an open grate in the floor right above the stove pipe that stretched across the living room and it supplied some heat to the upstairs. It also served as a good listening post when company was being entertained downstairs, especially when the school trustees held meetings there. The children slept together in double beds so this helped to keep them warm.

It was a very dry summer that year and the prospects of a good crop were poor. As it turned out the crop was very meager and, in fact, there was barely enough wheat to take to the mill in Inisfree to be ground into flour. However they did manage to get five 100 pound bags, enough to make bread, cakes and cookies for the winter. Helen became a very good cook and was always taking a new recipe from the huge Mrs. Beaton's cookbook she brought from England. With the flour came bran, shorts, and cream of wheat. The bran was used in cooking, the shorts was added to the cow feed, and the cream of wheat made good porridge for the breakfast table. Helen made at least one big batch of bread every week once the family grew in number. Helen enjoyed cooking so long as the wood box was kept full of dry wood for the stove. She became an expert at adjusting the dampers on the stove to get exactly the right temperature in the oven for baking.

The Rayments always had a very large vegetable garden and they could store much of it in the cellar to last all winter.

It was usual to have fifteen or twenty gunny sacks of potatoes in the bin to feed hungry mouths.

During the year 1922 word was received that Helen's father had passed away in England. The decision was made that Grandma Yeatman would come to Canada and live on the farm with Helen and Albert. Now this was going to require some major changes. She would come after the arrival of the new baby and some renovations were done to accommodate her. She had a bit of money and Albert hired a carpenter to make the changes. The main bedroom downstairs would be her room and Albert and Helen would move upstairs into the south bedroom. They also had a small toilet closet built into the bedroom so that Grandma didn't have to go outside. The toilet consisted of a pail with a seat on it [commode] and a vent pipe to the outside. A new heater was purchased for her room and she would have the benefit of a coal fire all winter. It was a cozy room facing south and with lace curtains on the bay window that looked down on what used to be a lake but was now a big slough.

On April 12 Helen woke Albert and told him the time had come to go to the hospital. The roads were in dreadful condition; half snow and half mud but Albert hooked up the democrat and off they went on a treacherous journey to Viking. The last few miles were a nightmare. Albert thought he might have to help deliver a bay on the road. However they made it just on time. The baby, a girl was born just ten minutes after their arrival at the hospital. It became a neighborhood joke that anyone wanting to speed up the labor process just go for a ride in the democrat with Albert. He would make it to the hospital on time. They were back on the farm after a six day stay; a family of four. They named the baby Joyce. [No middle name] This meant more diapers. They were cut and hemmed from large sheets of flannelette and of course used over and over again. This also meant heating water on the stove for washing every couple of days. By the way; those diapers were also ironed with the flat iron. Those who could not afford flannelette used sugar sacks or flour sacks to make diapers.

The time was nearing for the arrival of Grandma. Albert got some congolium for the floors which made cleaning much easier and improved the look of the place. In doorways and other seams a narrow strip of brass was nailed down to hold it in place. Also a thin material called plaster board was applied to the downstairs rooms and some new curtain for the kitchen, and living room made a much cheerier home to live in.

At last the long awaited day arrived. Helen received a letter stating that her mother would be sailing on May 10, 1923 and that she would arrive in Minburn on May 20th. By the time the letter arrived she had already left and would be arriving in four days time. Albert and Helen were off in the democrat to meet the train on that day. What a joyous reunion it was when Grandma stepped off the train that day. When Albert saw what she had brought with her he knew that a trip would have to be taken in the wagon. She had three large steamer trunks and her crated piano; much more than could be loaded onto the democrat. Elizabeth Anne Yeatman was a small stately woman. As a child she had a tendon problem on one foot and she walked with a slow shuffling gait. There was nothing medical science could do about it at the time but she managed to get around adequately. Her waist length hair was worn in a bun at the back of her head giving her a stately appearance that seemed to demand respect.

Now came the time for adjustment to country life. Although she spent most of her life in a small town called Chichester near London, the farm seemed like total isolation. The neighbors kindly came over to have tea with her and to give her encouragement. Albert hitched up the wagon and went to Minburn to fetch the rest of Grandma's belongings. With the help of Angus Faulkner Albert was able to move the piano into the house and place it in the living room with the back to the stairwell wall where it stood as long as they were on the farm. The piano was terribly out of tune due to the long trip and climate change. It happened that a piano tuner traveling the country came across Sumersdale farm. He tuned up the piano and put her name in his notebook to call in once a year to keep the piano in tune. Grandma had funds to look after this. The doctor in England had prescribed a tot of brandy each day to ease the pain from rheumatism that frequently bothered her. She found out that she had to have a doctor's prescription to get a bottle of brandy because prohibition was in effect at the time. A couple of the neighbors would drop in periodically and ask after Grandma's health. Perhaps Grandma had a good supply of brandy on hand and she would let them use her prescription to get a bottle for themselves. The only other source of alcohol was moonshine or other concoctions made illegally at home. The R.C.M.P. was kept busy trying to track down stills that may be hidden in a straw pile. People were allowed to make wine for personal consumption and it was amazing to see what showed up under the name of wine. Anyhow Grandma's brandy supply was well looked after.

In 1924 it again became apparent that Helen was pregnant. The baby would be born in early September; probably in the midst of harvest time. The family was slowly filling up the space in the house. During winter was a difficult time if the baby was in the crawling stage because the floors were very cold. One day Albert came home with a rug for the living room and it must have been good quality because it was still there many years later. He also got a radio, battery operated, which opened up the news of the world to the home.

Many of the farmers worked a couple of weeks a year on road improvement. They built up grades and generally improved the roads to year around use. Quite a few of the farmers were getting cars and trucks so it was necessary to have better roads. Still they were dirt roads and when it rained they became a quagmire and people had to go back to the reliable horse.

As the summer wore on Helen became quite large and tired easily. Once again she hired Effie to help out. She was a very capable girl and the children adored her. She managed the cooking when the threshing crew came and kept the house in good order. Mrs. MacFarlane had offered to take Helen to hospital when the time came if the roads were dry. On September 11, 1924 the labor pains began. The weather was dry so she got a ride with Mrs. Mac [as she was known as]. The baby was born that day, a bouncing boy of 12lb 13 oz. What a joy to see such a robust child. They named the baby Hugh, after his father and Yeatman, after his mother's maiden name.

Albert was indeed a very busy man milking six cows, cutting wood for the fires, and all the other chores that keep a farm running smoothly. Helen had her hands full looking after three children, keeping the fires going, baking bread, and house cleaning. Grandma ironed clothes and mended, helped with the children but she stayed out of Helen's kitchen. Grandma also loved to play the piano and spent many hours knitting. Fred would soon be old enough to take piano lessons. They got two news papers from England [late]; the Daily Mirror and the Daily Sketch. The Free Press came from Winnipeg every week which gave the Canadian news.

As mentioned before, this part of the book will relate to the growing up of the Rayment children with particular attention being paid to Hugh Y. Rayment, the author of this book. Having established this, it would seem proper to refer to Hugh in the first person in the rest of the book.

My mother told me that I was a good baby which probably meant that I did not cry very much. As I grew older I had a growth spurt and became tall and thin; perhaps a little frail but was very active and sometimes a bit adventuresome. At one time father had a carpenter working in the house. When mother called them in for tea they left the ladder up and I climbed up onto the roof. When the men came out they were astonished to see me running around up there unaware of any danger. Father did not dare call out but sneaked up the ladder and rescued me.

On March 9th another baby boy joined the family. At that time the roads happened to be dry and Helen got a ride to Viking with Ena Revil. The Revils lived on the next farm south of us. The baby was named Alfred Keith. By this time mom and dad were getting quite concerned that the children had not been baptized. While in hospital she got in touch with the minister and made arrangements to have him come out to Rodino as there were a number of Anglican families there that had children and had not had the opportunity to get it done. One bright Sunday Rev. Bea came and was surprised to have 10 children and 2 adults to baptize. While he was there they asked him to include Rodino in the Viking parish and have a monthly service in the school. Strangely enough there was a pump organ in the school and either Grandma or Mother could play for the services. Rev. Bea agreed to talk to the Bishop and later that year the services were begun in the school. Ivy Daniel volunteered to hold weekly Sunday school lessons for the children and so it was that Rodino became quite a strong Anglican community. An adjoining district, Lake Alice also had a number of Anglican families and they also joined the Viking parish and had monthly services. The Rayments occasionally piled into the democrat or the model T and went over to Lake Alice for a service. They met the Wrights. Two brothers had married sisters and lived on adjoining farms. They became very good friends and visited back and forth for dinners and music around the piano.

It was about this time that telephone service became available and most of the farmers, including the Rayments, got hooked up to the line. It was a party line and everyone had their own ring. These phones are only found in museums now but they were a vital link in rural Alberta at that time. To phone somebody one had to know their ring which was operated by turning a crank on the side of the box; our ring 1 long and 2 shorts. They could even get long distance by pressing a button on the side of the box and giving one long ring. This connected with the operator in Minburn, Mrs. Cowell. She made the connection. Being a party line one could listen in other people's calls so there were very few secrets in the district.

There were times when the phone was used to alert people of an emergency situation. I remember a fire that was set by a young lad and it spread into a huge prairie fire, a constant fear because crops could be quickly be destroyed in the blaze. When an alarm was sent out by telephone all the neighbors rallied forth to fight the fire. Another emergency was when a child strayed from the farm and was lost. Everybody turned out on horseback and searched until the youngster was found. I remember one time when father went to town Joyce and I decided to follow him and we got hopelessly lost. We were found nearly a mile from home crying our eyes out in a wheat field.

About this time Albert came home with a Model T Ford car. It was a great improvement over the horse and buggy. It had a canvas top and side curtains with cellophane side windows. It had to be cranked to start it. In the winter the radiator had to be drained because there was no anti-freeze or block heaters in those times. Hot water was poured into the radiator to get it started for the next trip. It wasn't all that good a vehicle for winter because it had no heater and the sleigh could be made much more comfortable and reliable. The car was equipped with high pressure tires and it wasn't unusual to have one or more flats on a trip to town. The tire had to be removed from the rim and the inner tube removed and patched with rubber patches supplied in a kit. This took the biggest part of an hour – quite frustrating, particularly if it was raining.

On September the 8th, 1928 Kenneth Brian was born. The big room upstairs could accommodate three double beds so there was plenty of room for expansion. The business of feeding and clothing five children was quite a challenge. I remember large parcels of clothes coming from England to help out. These clothes were not exactly Canadian farm style but then other families got parcels too. I remember mother and father sitting down at the dining room table with Eaton's catalogue and making out the big order for winter clothes for all of us. We wore a lot of hand-me-downs but each of us got something new; maybe even a new winter coat. There was great excitement when the big parcel arrived from Eaton's. I also remember Grandma knitting me a pair of woolen shorts. They were a sort of caramel color and I hated them but had to wear them. My day of liberation came when I was sliding down the hill at school. A thread got caught on a piece of wire and to my delight the shorts unraveled beyond repair. This accident was looked upon with some doubt but it did get rid of those awful pants.

By the late twenties the older children were old enough to take on some of the chores, i.e. milking cows, feeding the stock, chopping wood, and helping mother in the house. I don't remember feeling hard done by. We all had to do our share and as each new responsibility was given us we took it on as a part of growing up.

Father was a very quiet man and the responsibility of punishing us for misdeeds fell to mother. A few whacks across the bare bottom usually did the trick. If nobody owned up to the misdeed she would have all of us bend over the kitchen bench with pants down and she would work down the line. It must have been very effective because it didn't happen very often. There was one thing that mother would not tolerate and that was talking back to Grandma. In fact respect for older people was expected and strictly enforced. Father was not beyond putting us in place if we annoyed him too much. It was just as well to stay out of his way if things were not going well; particularly if a piece of machinery broke down.

Grandma gave all of us piano lessons but I was not interested in the piano. I wanted a set of orchestra drums. I got a harmonica and managed to play a few tunes on it. One year I got a Jew's harp and made a lot of noise with it as well. There was another instrument called a Kazoo. And each of us got one for Christmas. I think Mother regretted giving us those noisy things.

**Chapter Three*

Christmas time was a very exciting time for all of us. A Christmas parcel always came from Grandpa Rayment in London. There was a gift for every one of us. The suspense was terrible because we knew we could not see the presents until Christmas Day and we got the parcel a week or two before Christmas.

Father went to town a day or two before Christmas and brought home a box of Japanese oranges, a big box of apples, some candy, and because evergreen trees did not grow in that part of the country, he brought home a Christmas tree from the railway station. He also had a load of coal to ease the chore of chopping wood at this time.

On Christmas morning the children were awake at a very early hour. They delved into their stockings to see what Santa had brought them. There was always an orange in the toe. Some candies, an apple, a small gift, and usually a lump of coal to take up any space that was left over. The gift from Grandpa was given out from the tree in the evening of Christmas Day.

The Rayments, Daniels, and the Johnstons always exchanged visits during the Christmas season. Each family cooked a huge turkey when their turn came to entertain.

Mother always made Christmas cakes and Christmas pudding for dinner. She poured a little bit of Grandma's brandy on the pudding and lit it just before serving.

Nobody had electric power so wax candles were placed in special holders that clipped onto the branches of the tree. They were all lit for the passing out of gifts. Father always had a bucket of water ready in case of fire. One of the fathers played Father Christmas and handed out the gifts. He was dressed in a Santa suit and we usually knew who it was. One year Father brought in some photography equipment to take a picture of everyone sitting in front of the tree. It consisted of his Kodak camera, a large flash bulb and a car battery. Everybody had to sit perfectly still. The shutter on the camera was opened and at the same moment a circuit from the battery to the bulb was closed. There was a huge flash and the picture was taken. The film had to be sent away for developing and it took a week or two to get the pictures back. Some of these pictures may be seen in our family albums today

Mother always made Turkish delight for the festive season. The ingredients were poured into flat pans until set and then icing sugar was sprinkled on it and it was cut into squares for serving—delicious. We also made ice cream for Christmas. The ingredients were poured into a container which was set in a pail of ice and salt. It was mixed until stiff and then set out in a snow drift to keep cold. I remember one year a couple of Johnston's dogs followed them over to our house. They got into the ice cram and ate the works.

Most families had a patch of ice cleared of snow on a nearby slough and to use up some of the energy we were sent outside to skate. Sometimes there were a few frost bites but it did give the adults a chance to visit in peace. Just think of it; there would be about ten kids at each gathering; all excited about Christmas!! To round out the celebration we would all gather around the piano and sing carols to Grandma's accompaniment. Around midnight the guests would pile into the sleigh and off home to bed.

The 1930's, also known as "the dirty thirties" many Canadians were out of work. They roamed the country looking for any kind of work they could get.. The prairies suffered unprecedented hot weather and drought. I remember us all watching the western sky for signs of rain clouds. The farmers were not too badly affected because we had plenty of meat and vegetables. We ate wild mushroom and puff balls that were quit plentiful. We picked leaves off the common pigweed and mother cooked it up as greens. It was quite tasty with poached eggs. Of course we had plenty of meat. I recall Mother saying, "Go and wring a chicken's neck for dinner" Because of the shortage of money we didn't often get new clothes. We went bare foot in the summer to save on footwear. Strangers sometimes wandered through our district and often would cut wood for a meal. There were no locks on the doors. One time we were out, when we got home a man was splitting firewood for us. He had come in the house and made himself a meal. He thanked us and was on his way. A few of them got hired by local farmers and just worked for room and board.

There was usually an abundance of wild berries and mother sent us out to pick them. Saskatoons were the most plentiful and Mother gave us a milk pail each and told us not to come back until they were full. One time I wanted to go hunting with a friend but Mother insisted that I fill a pail with saskatoons before I could go. I went to the berry patch and filled the pail half full of leaves and put berries on the top. I took them home and then made a hurried departure. I got immediate gratification but when I got home it was a different story.

Mother, like all other farmers' wives had to learn how to preserve food for the winter. She wasn't satisfied until there were at least 300 jars of canned fruit on the cellar shelves. Most of it was wild fruit. We grew marrows in the garden and they made wonderful deserts. They were peeled, hollowed out, and the meaty part was cut into cubes and preserved like fruit. Mother added a bit of ginger root for extra flavor. We all liked it so she preserved many jars of it. We had some bushes of red and white currents in the garden. They produced plenty of fruit to make jellies and jams.

Most of the farmers in north and central Prairies did not suffer too badly from the depression but in the south it was a different story. It was so dray that the farm soil literally blew away. It drifted over the fences. The livestock grew thin and many died of starvation. Many of these farmers just loaded what belongings they could load into their wagons and abandoned their farms. Many moved to the Peace River district where new land was available and they made a new start. Most were successful and enjoyed a prosperous life. Others collected relief, a form of welfare, from the Government. Many were too proud to accept it and just suffered it out.

In the spring of 1930 Mother discovered that she was once again pregnant. When father heard of it he was said to have thrown his hat on the ground and jumped on it. I don't think he was jumping for joy. The new baby would arrive in the dead of winter and the roads would probably be drifted in. Mrs. Tommy volunteered to act as midwife and the baby could be born at home. The only thing I remember about it was it being strange that Mother moved into Grandma's room and Grandma moved upstairs. On Boxing Day Mrs.

Tommy came over and disappeared into the bedroom with Mother. We didn't know what was going on but Fred peaked in the window and said he saw a bay in there. This episode upset the Christmas celebrations but we all took it in stride and welcomed the new member of the Rayment family. He was named Thomas after Mr. Daniel and Alleyne after a favorite cousin of Mothers. With six children the house was certainly filled to near capacity.

By this time a new batch of settlers came to the district. They were brought out from England by the Hudson Bay Company and each settled on a quarter section of Bay land. Four families moved in on a section one mile south of us. Laidlers were on one quarter and Beckets were next to them. Winfields and Freemans took the other two quarters. They had children and Rodino School now was filled to capacity. Their children were born in England and in their teens, At times Mother would hire one of the girls to help out at harvest time. One time Rosie Becket came to look after us while Mother and dad were away. Rosie decided to make a cake. Being a bit mischievous, I put salt in the sugar container. You can imagine what that cake was like. Bob Johnston was coming over and he always helped himself to whatever there was to eat on the counter. We made sure to leave some of this out for him. Sure enough he came into the kitchen and helped himself to a big piece of cake and took a big bite of it. I don't think we even got a slap for that one.

How well I remember the Sundays we went to Church at Rodino or Lake Alice or Viking. Dad designed and drew the plans for the Church in Viking. There was a regular routine for preparing to go to Church. On Saturday night we all had a weekly bath in the big round tub. The water was heated on the stove and we all bathed in the same water. On

Sunday morning we dressed in our best clothes, polished our shoes, and got a good hair brushing. After a final inspection we were loaded into whatever vehicle we were going in and off we went. The children were given strict orders to remain silent during the service. Whichever place we went there was always a big meal after the service. If at our house Mother usually cooked a roast and made Yorkshire pudding with thick gravy to top it off.

In the summer, if there was no service we all went to Camp Lake, about five miles from our place. We had a good swim and then a picnic afterwards. The water in the lake was about the color of lemonade and very nice to bathe in. Of course we went for a dip in the big slough at home but the water was anything but clean. All the same we made a raft and had a great time there.

Springtime was a wonderful time of year. As the sun got warm we could shed our winter clothes and play outside. It was a competition to see the first robin or crow returning from the south. Very soon the crocuses were popping up through the snow. We became great engineers rerouting streams and making big puddles that would freeze over and we could skate on them. We had tame ducks and they for some reason laid eggs in the slough. We would gather them up and although they were too strong to eat fresh, Mother did use them in cooking. Later the ducks laid their eggs in nests and hatched the cutest little ducklings. When the gophers came out of hibernation we got busy snaring them and removing their tails. There was a bounty on them because of the damage they did to the crops. We got a cent apiece for the tails.

Father set aside a five acre portion of his land for a sports field and every summer people from all around came and took part in the festivities. They had ball games, foot races, horse races, and many other fun games for children and adults alike. There were booths set up with lemonade, ice cream, candies, and other goodies. This is where we spent our gopher tail money. Everybody went home for evening chores and then crowded into the school for a dance. This was the main highlight of the season.

Chapter Four

In the early 1930's a drilling rig moved in a mile north of us in search of oil. They constructed a wooden derrick and started drilling. A couple of small houses were built nearby to house the field superintendent and the engineer with their families. I don't think any of us really knew what was going on there but we watched with wide eyed interest as the huge engine roared day and night. One day we heard a terrific roar and, looking to the north, we saw a huge pawl of smoke high in the sky over the site. Debris was flying up and flames joined the mix. They had struck natural gas and it gushed up with tremendous force. It took about ten days to extinguish the flames and finally the well was capped and everything calmed down. There were large timbers scattered over an area of about 20 acres. Father gathered a load of these and hauled them home. He cut them into lengths for fence posts and some of them still stand today. Once the well was secure the super-intendent, Charlie Mills and his family moved away. Harry Manning, the engineer stayed on as caretaker of the well. The two houses had natural gas piped in for heat and light. Dan and Clara Laidler moved into the vacated house. He worked for Tommy Daniel for years as his hired man. He ran the threshing crew at harvest time. Clara had two boys from a previous marriage to Dave Elliot who was killed in a railway crossing accident. Dan and Clara had a daughter, Elaine.

Harry Manning was a very ambitious man. He had his tractor converted to use natural gas and ran a chopping mill for the farmers. They came from far and wide because Harry charged very little for the service. He was also very community spirited and he built a regulation size hockey rink. There was a gas heated skate change shack and a small concession where he sold chocolate bars; 5 cents and other goodies to the kids. Young lads from the district made up a hockey team and they played other teams from the area. They did very well though I don't remember any trophies being won. There was always a crowd looking on from the snow banks around the rink. Harry liked entertaining the kids and made sure they had plenty of rink time. He set up a skate sharpening service at 5 cents per skate. My brothers and I walked that mile many Saturdays to free skate or play a bit of hockey. We could skate all day for a dime. I had a second hand pair of skates that were held onto my shoes by clamps. It was years before I got a pair of Bauer tube skates. As a matter of fact I still have them. They are probably suitable for the museum now.

Harry died suddenly from a heart attack and the house and the job were taken over by the Lever family. Gertie Lever had two children, a boy, Dennis, and a girl, Patsy. Gertie's parents, Mr. and Mrs. Baldwin lived with them at the gas well.

We were great hockey enthusiasts and never missed Foster Hewitt's Hockey Night in Canada. I knew every Toronto Maple Leaf player by name and number and idolized every one of them. They played clean hockey in those days and for modest pay. It was a sport. Some people didn't have radios and they would come to our house to listen to the games. We also listened to the heavy weight boxing matches. Joe Louis was our hero. Our house was full on those nights as well. Mother would make up a big jug of cocoa and some cinnamon buns with raisins or baking powder biscuits with jam. Those were unforgettable times.

Adults gathered at least once a month at the school house to play whist. People came from all around and if they didn't have someone to baby-sit they brought their babies with them and bedded the down around the heater. There was great competition and it was a great pass-time to wile away the winter. A couple of times during the winter box socials were held at the school. This was usually a fund raiser for some worthy cause. A few romances developed from these events. There was always a school concert put on by the kids. A curtain was hung on a wire across the back of the room for a stage. I remember one fateful concert when I was in grade two. I was chosen to make a short recitation. I went through the procedure just fine but when I finished I forgot to bow. Allan Faulkner who was operating the curtain didn't know I was finished and left me standing there for what seemed like an hour before he finally closed the curtain. As always, there was a Christmas tree after the show and Santa came and every child got a gift. This night Santa came and all of the children got their gifts except me. I was noticed crying after Santa left and a search was made of the tree and my gift was found. It was a coloring book and crayons and although I accepted the gift, I hated that coloring book and it was a long time before I even looked at it.

We could never stay too late at the school functions because the home fires had to be stoked or everything would freeze up. There were very few homes that had any insulation so it didn't take long to get cold when the fires died down. There were two great fears concerning fires. One was that the fires may go out in time of illness and there was nobody to stoke them. The other was that the fire would get out of control and burn the house down. Both incidents occurred in our district. The Paul family lost their home to fire on a very cold night in December. The family got out all right but they had to take refuge in with neighbors. Two of the Paul children stayed with us over Christmas. The community held dances and other events to raise money to get the Paul family into another home. People came forward with clothes, blankets, and other household items to help out the Paul's. Farm people are very generous in the case of such an emergency.

As mentioned there was a pump organ at the school and it provided some of the music for dances. On occasion Grandma even came to the school to play. She had difficulty with the pedals because of her disability. I remember getting down and pumping the pedals for her by hand. A few other members of the community could play an instrument and did their bit to add to the entertainment. Rodino did not yet have a community hall so the school had to serve the purpose. It was around1935 when Bill Revill donated ten acres of land two miles south of us for a community center. Everybody pitched in and a hall was built on the property. This was a boon to the community. Dances were held on most Saturday nights 8:00 to 12:00 PM. Friday night dances went to 2 or 3 in the morning. The orchestra played to 1:00 AM and then the people would take up a collection for more dancing. In the cold winter nights, those who drove cars had to drain their radiators to prevent freezing up and at the end of the dance they took water from the stove, melted snow, and refilled the radiators. There were no block heater or anti-freeze in those days. One night Bill Johnson found there was no more hot water left so he used the left over coffee in his model T. It didn't seem to do any harm.

About this time the gas lamp came on the market. It gave off a very strong white light and soon replaced the coal oil lamp. Mother still longed for electric lights. Eaton's advertised a wind charger in their catalogue and Father sent away for one. Douglas Bevan, our teacher helped father to install it on the roof of the house. It was a six volt outfit and did produce good light as long as the wind blew. However it was only good for lighting and would not run an electric motor. We had six big storage batteries in our bedroom and I can still hear them bubbling away as they charged. Also Mother sent away to Eaton's for gas operated iron. It burned white gas and was very efficient and saved firing up the stove in the hot summer days. She also got a new washing machine. It had a wooden tub and a dolly mounted in the lid. A handle on the side had to be moved back and forth by hand to activate the dolly and wash the clothes. There was also a hand operated wringer mounted on a stand between two rinse tubs. This took the place of the scrub board and a great deal of drudgery on wash day. Later on this machine was replaced by a copper tub Beatty washing machine with a gasoline engine on it. A hole was punched in the wall to run the exhaust pipe outside. It was noisy but reduced the workload even more. Were we getting modern – or what?

We lived only a quarter of a mile from the school so we rarely took our lunch. At 12:00 noon we would rush home in time to hear Ma Perkins and Pepper Young's Family on the radio, eat lunch, and rush back to school before the bell. Another thing I loved to listen to was cowboy music sung by such stars a Wilf Carter and Rod MacLeod, Alberta's Singing Cowboy. I still find myself humming those tunes.

Douglas Bevan was a great teacher. He was strict but fair and everybody liked him. Our soft ball team very seldom won a game so Mr. Bevan told us we had to learn to catch the ball. He took each one of us separately and stood us in front of the school barn and threw the ball at us until we did learn to catch it. He also taught us a few strategies of the game and we beat every school in the district after that. He was also a very good mechanic and took it on himself to overhaul dad's model T Ford. He wouldn't take any money for his labor. He left our school in 1940 to join the RCAF. He was stationed in Gander, Newfoundland and was ferrying bombers to England. His plane went down in the Atlantic and he was never found. He had left his mark on all of us who attended his classes.

There was a soft ball game followed by a dance every Saturday night at the hall in the summer months. A bunch of us would meet at our gate and race the two miles to the hall. Sometimes there were two or even three on a horse. We were off in a cloud of dust at break-neck speed. And it is a wonder that nobody got killed. When Father got to hear about it he strictly forbid us from racing and he meant it.

One Saturday Henry Becket came over to see me. He had a new horse. It was a big boney gelding; sort of ugly in my view. However Henry was pretty proud of it and bragged about how fast it could run. Not to be outdone, I told him that our Jeff could outrun anything he could bring around. Father was away to town so I challenged Henry to a race. I got Jeff out of the barn and we went out to the road and measured off a half mile of good road for the race. My brother Ken acted as starter and away we went. Jeff was a race wise horse and started crowding Henry's horse. I saw Henry starting to slide off and tried to pull Jeff over. It was too late. We were riding bare-back and Henry went down under the horse, its hoof landing in his belly. When I got back to Henry he was rolling in pain. His first words to me were, "Don't tell my dad". Like me he would be in trouble if his parents knew he was racing. After all we were only 11 and 12 years old. Jim Laidler came along with his wagon and he took Henry on board and took him home. On Monday morning I waited anxiously for Henry to come to school. When he got there he said that he still had a lot of pain and that he had blood in his urine. He eventually got better and the secret didn't get out for years.

We often played tricks on one another as kids and one night the joke turned out to be on me. It was dark out and Fred was coming from the barn with a pail of milk. I grabbed a sheet off the clothes line and put it over me and stated to move toward him on my hands and knees. He let out a scream and threw the pail at me, drenching me with milk. I got into big trouble, first for dirtying the sheet and second for wasting the precious milk.

Once in a while a bird would get into the granary and we would climb up into the rafters and try to catch it. On one such occasion Fred fell and was knocked unconscious. Dad put a stop to that sort of thing. Being so far from a Doctor gave our parents a good deal of concern. As a little tyke Fred was playing around one of the horses and got stepped on and his leg was broken. When Alfred was a toddler he liked to chase the chickens. One day he was confronted by a big red rooster. The rooster retaliated and gave Alfred a good working over. He didn't chase chickens any more.

We had many ways of amusing ourselves in our spare time. In the summer we played such games as tag, anti I over, red light or just a good game of soft ball with our friends. In the winter we played fox and geese, sliding down the hill, skating, or just a good old snow ball fight. Later on we got skis for

Christmas. There were no ski boots; just a strap over whatever footwear we had on. We even built up a ramp of snow and jumped quite high. It is a wonder none of us broke our necks. We went most everywhere on those skis. It was much easier than trudging through deep snow.

Rodino had a fine little orchestra that played for most of the dances at the hall. Harry Johnston played the accordion, Abby Winfield played the drums, Cogy Christiansen played the piano, and her husband Axel played the violin. Sometimes mother took a turn at the piano. Although Grandma didn't play at the hall she was a great help at teaching these musicians the music for such pieces as "Red River Valley", "Spinning Wheel", and many more of the popular pieces of the time. As mentioned, Father later joined the orchestra with the saxophone. For special dances we usually hired Horenick's orchestra from Viking.

It was about this time, 1935 that the new Church was to be built in Viking. Mother got the brain wave to produce a play in the new hall to raise funds for the Church. She chose, of all things, Shakespeare's "A midsummer Night's Dream". Now this was a huge undertaking. Costumes had to be made and the scenery had to be produced in pastels on large panels. The Asses head had to be made and a cast put together. Many of the people were from Britain and had some cultural background. Bob Johnston plaid Pyrimus, Father played Thisbe, Tommy Daniel played Wall, Joyce played Puck, and the imps were played by the children, me included. Mother did the scenery on panels of building paper mounted on frames made by Father. Hours of practice was done at our house. Grandma helped out making the costumes. Most off them were made from old clothing and dyed for the right colors so there was very little outlay of cash. Finally the play was performed to a full house with howling applause. It was so successful that Mother booked to perform at Minburn and Viking.

Following this a group in Viking headed by Mr. and Mrs. Cary decided to put on an operetta, Gilbert and Sullivan's, "Trial by Jury" with Father taking a part. This was also a great success and enough money was raised to assure the building of the new Church, St. Mathew's Anglican Church. Following Trial by Jury they did, "HMS Pinafore" to finish the Church

With these successes Mother again decided to try a more modern comedy, "Black Cats". This again was a great success and was performed in the three locations. Amid all this activity Mother ran the Church bazaar, kept up with washing clothes, baking, and all the other household chores as well as feeding a large family. One would wonder how she did it.

In the spring of 1936 tragedy struck. Grandma had a dizzy spell and fell down the cellar stairs and broke her wrist. In great pain she was taken to Viking hospital where the bone was set and a cast put on. Shortly after that she had a stroke and paralyzed her left side. Her health continued to deteriorate and one day she sank into a coma. She remained at home and again Mrs. Tommy nursed her. She practically lived on barley water. She remained in the coma for nearly a year and all of us pitched in to attend to her needs. A lot of it was done by Joyce. One afternoon Fred was practicing the piano. All of a sudden we heard a call from Grandma, "That's the wrong note". From that day on she continued to get better. Although confined to her home-made wheel chair she took up needlepoint and other sewing; a marvelous lady indeed. Mother made her a sturdy fabric seat with a loop on each side and two poles could be passed through the loops and two people could transport her to the car or other places. She was with us for many years to come.

Children on the farm became useful at a very young age,. At 6 years old we could milk cows, chop wood; feed the animals, and many other chores. Everything was done for good of the farm. We were also very inventive. With few resources we had to improvise. Fred and I took on a project to solve the problem of the chickens eating their eggs. We took a two-compartment orange box and cut 2 inches off the bottom of the divider. One side of the box had a lid on it and the other side was open for the nest. That side was raised up so that when the hen laid her egg it would roll into the other compartment and we could collect the eggs at leisure. It worked so well that we converted all the nests and had no more trouble with losing eggs. We even sent the plans in to the farm page in the Winnipeg Free Press where it was published. We didn't apply for a patent so there was no reward other than our own satisfaction.

Another way of earning money was doing the janitor work at the school. It paid $5.00 a month which was not bad at the time. The job consisted of sweeping the floors of the school and the boy's and girl's outhouses, cleaning blackboards, and keeping the water cistern full of clean water from the school well. The cooler had to be emptied every night in the winter time or it would freeze solid. The janitor had to light the school fire at 6:00 AM to get the room warm for school at 9:00AM. Coal and wood had to be brought in from a shed in the barn. Once the fire was banked up with coal it was time to rush home, do chores, and eat breakfast before rushing back in time for the morning bell. The Faulkner kids had the job for a number of years and then we got it. When it came around to my turn I couldn't wait to get my first check.

I had been looking at a pair of Shiny black oxford shoes in Eaton's catalogue for weeks and wanted a pair. The price was $4.95 including a can of black shoe polish. That's what I got with my first check. When I got them I shined them over and over again. These were much better than the farm work boots to wear to the dances. I made sure the girls noticed them.

Speaking of footwear, it was the fashion to wear rubber boots over felt socks in the winter months. Other warm footwear included rubber boots over lumber sock or just plain moccasins. The important thing was to keep the feet dry in cold weather. Grandma taught all of us to knit and we spent many winter nights knitting scarves, socks, and mitts. We got very proficient at it and it kept the clothing bill down.

Young people of this era were hard workers, devoted to their responsibility to the family, to the animals, and eager to grow into adulthood. Their upbringing was reasonably strict and they knew that the chores had to be consistently done on time. If one were ill or for some reason couldn't their chores, the others had to fill in and would expect the same in return. In contrast, today's youth complain, "There's nothing to do", or, "It's boring". Those of us who went through those days on the farm find it hard to accept these complaints. We made our own entertainment such as sports, reading, music, or just making up games.

Young people rarely dated until in their late teens; girls didn't wear makeup or wear silk stockings till they were sixteen. There was a seam up the back of girl's stockings and those seams had to be straight. Above the knee skirts or dresses were out of the question. With the strict discipline at home and at school, teen pregnancies were very seldom seen. If a girl did become pregnant she usually "went to stay with an aunt" or some other excuse for her absence from school. The baby was usually adopted out or placed in an orphanage and the event went unnoticed.

There was very little crime committed by youth. Most boys drove cars by age fourteen because, after all, most of them could operate a tractor and other farm machinery by then. There were few car accidents because cars did not go very fast and road conditions were not conducive to speed. Most accidents involved slipping off greasy roads into the ditch in wet weather or running into livestock on the road. Cars had mechanical brakes that were not always in good working conditions. In wet weather the car wheels carved deep ruts in the road and when they dried out the car could slip into the ruts and take over the steering. When it jumped out it could mean a trip into a ditch. This was even worse when snow came and hid the ruts.

Although the technology of farming has advanced greatly since the early days, the basic rules of farm management still prevail. Through years of experience, farmers learned that cropping a piece of land in the same crop year after year would deplete the soil and the yields would drop yearly. They learned to rotate crops and every three or four years give the land a year of rest as fallow. It also allowed time to cultivate for weed control.

For the best result the farmer selected his best grain for Seed or bought registered seed. His own seed, he put through a fanning mill to remove unwanted weed seeds and other debris. He then treated the grain with formaldehyde or Ceresin as protection against grain diseases such as smut. The seed grain was poured into the seed drill and planted in the field. In the 1930's another crop infestation called rust attacked the wheat fields. Reddish orange spots formed on the blades and when harvested great clouds of red dust settled on everything and the crop was very poor, A new wheat seed 222 came out that resisted most of the crop diseases and since then many more improved strains have come on the market. This is thanks to the experimental farms that were set up on the prairies.

This did not affect the weather patterns that faced the farmers. There were such hazards as late frosts in the spring or early frosts in the fall. They were also subject to hail, drought, and heavy downpour of rain or, in some cases, tornadoes. Any one of these could reduce a crop of grain to zero production. Farming was always a gamble but these farmers were steadfast in their efforts to succeed. In the 1930's there were several consecutive years of drought and at the same time a world-wide depression. In the southern part of the prairie provinces it was so severe that many of the farmers had to take what belongings they could load into a wagon and abandon their farms. Some moved to the Peace River District where they got homestead rights and started afresh on the fertile soil of that area. Most of them eventually prospered and had good lives. Others moved to the cities and had to live on a meager Government allowance known as relief. Many were too proud to accept this handout and managed as best they could on what odd jobs they could find. Some starved to death. In spite of this the farmers of the Rodino district managed to hang on and raise their families.

My father had a huge stock book he brought from England. It listed all of the known stock diseases and the remedies. I spent many hours reading that book. Some of the cures of the day would seem very strange today, for instance, a horse developing a severe case of diarrhea may be treated with a good dose of red liniment mixed with water. A twitch was placed on the horse's ear which made it raise its head and the concoction was poured down its throat. It Worked!!   Epson salts administered in the same way, was a remedy for a number of ailments. When a horse got a sore on its shoulder from the collar rubbing on it a salve was applied. To ease the discomfort a piece of the collar was cut out so that it didn't rub when the horse was working. The same salve was used on the cow's teats when the got chapped. So this marvelous remedy, usually purchased from the Rawley's man was always in good supply in our barn. Father was very particular about the handling of his animals and would not stand for any mistreatment of them.

When Fred was sixteen he got a job with a neighboring farmer and got $40.00 a month plus room and board. I was next in line, thirteen, and figured I should have a job as well. I pleaded with my parents to let me go and they finally let me got to work for two brothers with the promise that, if the work were too much for me, I would come home. So I went to work for them and soon found out that they expected far more from me than a full grown man. It was haying time and very hot. I was put to work on the hay rake which was easy but they also expected me to stack the hay as the brought it in with the bucking pole. This is back breaking work and after eight hours of that I had to milk six cows before supper, One day I was on the rake in a dried up slough. The rake was just about worn out and the harness on the horses was patched with hay wire. One of the line came loose and I got off and went around in front of the horses to retrieve it. I had to lean over the neck yoke to reach it. I must have stopped on a wasp's nest and they were swarming around the horses hoofs. Suddenly they took off at a gallop. The rakes came down and I was trying to hang on. I knew I was going to fall and when I did I hooked my arm into one of the single trees and was being dragged on my butt. In a desperate effort I reached up and grabbed a line and pulled the team into a tight circle till they stopped. The two brothers reamed me out for not handling the team properly. At supper time I told them that I was needed at home and would not be back. They tried to do me out of some of my pay. I told them to pay my dad and they gave me the proper amount right away. So much for that experience!

On my return home I was told that a neighbor, Joe Swayne had been killed in a runaway with a team of horses. The Swaynes had come to Canada from Ireland and settled in the Rodino district three miles from our house. There were three brothers and two sisters, Carol, Joe, Mike, Onnie, and Kate. Carol was the eldest brother and he had last word in any decision regarding farm matters. Joe was more politically inclined, and mike was a very jolly man. He always had an Irish joke to tell. We learned to laugh at them even if they didn't make sense. The sisters worked very hard to keep the house and prepare scrumptious meals. Their barns were built from logs and had sod roofs. The house was very well built using lumber from the mill. Mike asked dad if I could come and work for them to take Joe's place. They paid me $45.00 a month plus room and board. It was a great place to work as long it was done the Irish way.

Mike took me in hand and treated me like an old country apprentice which meant doing everything the Irish way, including my social life. About this time I had started to notice girls and especially the Scott's hired girl Connie on the next farm. I borrowed Mike's saddle horse and met Connie at the gate and we went to the Saturday night dance at the hall. Of course I escorted her home. Apparently Mike saw us meet and ride off together. He confronted me in the morning, giving me a tongue lashing for chasing girls at my young age, threatening to send me home to my parents in disgrace. I enjoyed working there in spite of this and was well treated by all of them.

Mike had a registered bull that was kept in a coral near the barn. One morning Mike handed me a scythe and told me to go down to a nearby slough and cut a fork full of hay for the bull and I had to haul it up a very steep hill over my shoulder. I did this for a few days and then asked Mike, "Why don't we cut a load with the mower and haul it up to the yard in the hay rack"? I thought he was going to break a blood vessel as he roared at me, "That bull must have fresh hay every day". That was that!! The Swaynes wouldn't have a tractor on their fields because they said that it would spoil the land so all work was done with horses or by hand.

There was a very good well by the house except that the water intake to the pump was in very sandy soil and the leather valves wore out quite frequently and had to be replaced. This meant pulling the pump up to get at the cylinder. This was done with the use of a block and tackle mounted on a tripod. Mike had a very short tripod made up of three poplar poles tied together at the top with a logging chain. One hot summer morning Mike mentioned that the pump would have to be pulled. He went to town that day and I decided to pull the pump. A neighbor and school chum of mine, Stuart Daniel came over to see me and we decided to make a decent tripod so that the job could be done in half the time. There were some big tall poplar trees in a bush near the house so cut down three of them and made a grand tripod. We could now get the pump pulled up in three grabs rather than six or seven. We had the job finished before lunch time. When Mike came home he was astonished that the pump was fixed but furious when he saw the poles we used to make the tripod. There were other instances where I did things in a more practical way, saving labor. By and by Mike seemed to accept my ways and got to trust me with other projects. Another time we were harvesting the wheat. Mike ran the binder and I did the stooking. The binder kept kicking out loose bundles which meant that I had to tie them, using wheat stalks in place of twine. This made the job of stooking very slow and tedious. One day Mike had to go away for the afternoon on business and he told me to put the horses in the barn and continue stooking. I was determined to find out what was wrong with the binder so as soon as Mike was gone I set to work. I took the knotter off and found that the knife blade was very dull so that it just tore at the twine rather than cutting it. The bill hook was seized on to the bearing and the whole thing turned in the casting. I took that apart and cleaned it up and got some lubrication into it. It probably hadn't been oiled since the binder was new. When I finished getting it all back together I got on the binder and did three rounds on the field. It worked perfectly. When Mike came home he was amazed that such a young lad could fix anything as complicated as a knotter.

By this time I figured I was a man and, indeed, Mike bragged about his hired man. He often went to town on Saturday afternoon and one day he asked me if I would like to come along so away we went. He gave me ten dollars, part of my pay and I bought a new pair of gloves, a shirt, and a can of Dominion tobacco and papers. After milking the cows I went home for a visit. When I got home I went into the house and tossed the tobacco can on the table in full view of Mother and Father. Both of them used their psychology and completely ignored it. This knocked the wind out of my sails and I don't remember enjoying one smoke out of that can. It was a number of years before I took up the habit. I worked on there for the rest of the summer and then had to go back home. This had brought me through a, sometimes conceived, difficult time of life with little difficulty. I was growing tall and thin but strong.

That fall I went to work on Tommy Daniels threshing crew. I had to plead with mother and dad to let me go. Finally they said I could go if I promised to phone home if it was too much for me and they would send Alfred to help me. No reflection on Alfred but I would have died in the field before going to the phone. The work was very hard but I hung in there. One day when we were threshing at Daniel's home place an unfortunate thing happened. The machine was set up in a dried up slough bottom. It was very rough in there and just as I was pulling a load in the rack started to tip toward the machine. The front right axle was broken and over it went dumping bundles on to the main drive belt. It shot a couple of bundles forward and scared the team on the grain wagon. They bolted. Luckily enough the straw boss was sitting on the tractor and he shut the machine down before any more damage was done. The season ended with a big snow storm and then it was back to school for me in the middle of October.

As soon as school was out at the end of June I was back working at the Swaynes. They were happy to see me and Mike seemed much more tolerant with me this time around. We worked through the routine of farm work, plowing, haying, repairing fences, and into harvest. One morning I came down for breakfast and all of them were at the table and crying. I asked Mike what was wrong and he said, "Come with me". He led me into the kitchen and handed me a Luger hand gun and three bullets. He said "Yesterday afternoon I ran into Shas, their beautiful dog, with the binder and cut off his legs. Go down the field and put him out of his misery". This was one of the hardest tasks of my life. I loved that dog but I went down the field and did what Mike had bid me to do. There was no work that day. The family held a small burial service under a big tree at the end of the field.

When Billy Revil's threshing crew came Mike put me to work hauling grain from the separator to the granary. Now this was back breaking work. He had two wagons and when one was full I hitched the team on to it and hauled it to the granary and unloaded it into the bin with a grain scoop. It had to be lifted over my head into the grain door. As soon as it was unloaded I had to rush back to the separator and take the waiting load to the granary. At the end of the day I was very tired and when I came to the house for supper the women handed me the milk pails and said, "Those poor cows haven't been milked yet".

When the threshing was done Billy Revil asked me if I would come and work for him on his threshing crew. I spoke to Mike about it and he told me that the money I would get would be more than he could pay so I made the switch. This was the start of a span of three years on his crew and I also worked full time for him for one winter. In the meantime I had to continue with my education and so took correspondence courses, working on them in the bunk house at nights. Billy had a 16 volt wind charger which supplied his lighting requirements for all the buildings, including the bunk house. When the wind died down and the batteries got low I had to resort to the coal oil lamp. I did very well on the three courses. That year the snow had come early and halted the threshing for the season. Billy had some crop still out and in January decided to continue the harvest. This was extremely hard work because the butts of the bundles were frozen into the ground and were hard to get loose. However we got the job done. We also threshed a stack of flax for the Winfield's. This was tough too because of the dampness and the flax kept winding around the cylinder and plugging the machine. This meant shutting down and cutting it loose with a knife.

One day I noticed an ad in the paper showing pop corn seed for sale and I Thought, "Wow!! What a way to make some money", and I sent away for some seed. I put it in the ground and waited for a big crop. It was a very dry year and we got hail. The net result was a very meager crop so the fortune I was looking forward to fizzled out. However we did get enough pop corn for family use. With good conditions I still think it could have been a worthwhile project. I left the farm and so it was never pursued.

Chapter Five

At age fifteen I was still skinny as a rail but strong and wiry. I could handle most of the farm work and was especially interested in anything mechanical. I was always asking my dad how things worked. And would tackle any repair job that I thought I could handle. One day Dad came home from town with a twelve foot 2x6. It was straight as a die and dad told me it was for a new drawbar for the harrows and, "Keep your hands off it". As soon as he was off to work in the field I set to work on the draw bar which meant taking all the hardware off the old one and installing on the new one. Half inch holes had to be drilled with a hand brace and bit in exactly the right positions and then the draw hooks bolted into place. I just got finished when dad came in from the field. When he saw it he was astonished and said, "I couldn't have done a better job myself.". He entrusted me to other mechanical jobs after that; even sharpening shears for the plough.

There were other jobs on the farm that I detested, mostly to do with the livestock. Once a year the bull calves had to be castrated and all the calves dehorned and branded. To me this was the height of cruelty. There was no anesthetic and the parts were washed with the disinfection, kreolin before the operation. For branding the irons were heated to red hot in the forge and then pressed into the animals hide to burn in the brand. The animals bawled with the pain but got over it in a few days. In later years the vet was called in to perform these duties and more humane methods were used.

Butchering a beast for our meat supply was another of those bad days. The animal was knocked out with a blow to the head with the back of the axe and then its throat was slit allowing it to bleed to death. It was then strung up on a tripod, skinned, disemboweled, and then allowed to hang for a few days before being cut up for use. This had to be done after freeze – up. There was no refrigeration so we stored the meat in the wheat in the granary to prevent spoilage. There was no refrigeration on the farm and the grain would keep the meat frozen until spring. Most of the farmers used this method. When spring came any meat that was left was brought in and Mother canned it for summer use. Every fall a man came around with a load of fish and we kept them in the grain too.

Somehow I knew that education was important and that if I were to ever get off the farm I would have get more than a grade nine education. My parents knew this and helped me get enrolled in correspondence courses. Of course Grandma was a great help. In 1939 I was in grade eight and that was the year WW2 broke out. One of the older boys quit school and joined the Army 3 days after Canada declared war. When he came home on leave he was the envy of all of us. Billy Revill was a first WW1 Veteran and he came to the school and gave the older boys, including myself. some basic drill. Father was talking about joining the Home Guard.

I dug right into my school work, knowing that I needed at least grade 10 to get into the air force. Still, as a young teenager, I wasn't beyond getting into a bit of mischief.. There was a big hornets' nest hanging in a tree just outside the school grounds. When it got cold enough the hornets stayed inside the nest in a dormant state. I and a buddy cut the nest down and placed it in a cupboard in the school. The next day, when the school got warmed up, the hornets came out in droves. The teacher was terrified and sent us all home. We knew this was big trouble. On the weekend the school got cold and the hornets went back into their nest and we were able to remove it from the school. If I remember correctly that was one of the rare occasions I got a few licks of the strap.

As the war news came over the radio we could see the stern looks on our parents faces. Most of them were of British decent and feared that the German forces would invade Britain. As the news became grimmer, more and more of the farm lads joined up, and farm labor was short handed. Young girls and boys became a significant part of farm work force.

When Winston Churchill became prime minister of Britain everybody listened to his words of encouragement and he was an instant hero.

At this time Fred was interested in a career in agriculture and attended the School of Agriculture in Vermillion. He was nearing military age and soon joined the RCAF. The country was transformed to a total war footing. Thousands of young women went to work in factories freeing young men for the military. There were girls working in the shipyards, aircraft factories, and many other facilities that were making war materials. There was a big demand for knitted scarves and socks for the troops. Grandma taught all of us to knit. Ladies got together and made bandages to be sent overseas.

I stayed home for the summer of 1940 and took on some of the farm work with Alfred. Ken was getting old enough to help out with the milking, chopping wood, and other chores. Father had seen an ad in the paper for a draftsman with the

Department of Transport. He applied and two gentlemen flew out to interview him. They landed at the farm and hired him on the spot. It was decided that mother would stay on the farm and we boys would run the operation. After all we had grown up with it and were quite capable of doing the work.

That winter Billy Revill phoned and wanted me to come to work for him for the winter. I told him that I had enrolled in three correspondence courses and he said that would be OK. I could work on them in the bunk house after all the chores were done. He had a 12 volt wind charger so I had electric light to work by except when there was no wind and then I had to revert to the coal oil lamp. Billy ran a big pig operation and one day he announced that it was castration day. Allen Faulkner and Pete Laidler came over and we castrated 100 pigs that day. Guess what!! We had sweetbreads for supper. Such is farm life!

By this time I had purchased a set of orchestra drums from Abby Winfield for $20.00 and a pig. Joyce and I took turns playing for Saturday night dances at the hall. We got $3.00 for a Saturday night dance that ended at midnight sharp. We got $5.00 for a Friday night dance that could go till 3:00AM plus a silver collection if it went on later than that. I must admit that I wasn't the greatest drummer but the folks didn't seem to mind so long as I kept in time with the music.

I was a member of the Young People's Society and attended their regular monthly meetings. Billy Revill was president and his wife Ena was secretary treasurer. They were great organizers and everybody was content to elect them year after year. Billy was very good at conducting meetings using proper parliamentary procedure. I envied him and hoped that some day I would be able to do the same. At the present I was too shy to think of putting my name down as a candidate.

Young people of the district learned a great deal from Billy and many went on to be successful farmers or on to careers of their choice.

Some people look down on farmers as not being very smart but I think they have a far better understanding of life than most. Many of them got no further than grade eight in the one-room school, yet they had a far better knowledge of life and certainly knew how to do a good days work. Much of the farming know-how was handed down from one generation to the next. Farmers had to make their own repairs to machinery and they had to be able to make wise decisions about when to seed and when to harvest. They also had to look after the livestock. It wasn't always possible to get the assistance of a vet. Most of the pioneer farmers came from Europe and had never lived on a farm. They had to start from scratch with very few resources and had to learn on the job. They should be rated as first class citizens.

In 1940 Fred went to Viking for a year of high school. He boarded at the Cary's. They didn't charge room and board but received meat and vegetables from the farm. I stayed on at Revill's through the winter and the following summer. After the harvest of 1941 I got the privilege of going to Viking for a year of high school and also stayed with the Cary's. By this time Fred was in the RCAF and I wanted to follow in his footsteps there as well. Before dad went away he made arrangements to have Angus Faulkner help out on the farm. Alfred, Ken, and Tom were able to handle the chores and I credit Alfred with making many of the farm decisions.

Once again I had to finish the harvest with Bill's threshing crew before starting school. I had a lot of catching up to do and dug right in to my studies. By this time the pecking order had been established with the boys and along with another farm boy the two leaders decided they would put us in place, It didn't take Arnold and I very long to show them who was who. Of course we had been well conditioned from the farm work and the town boys were no match for us. They left us alone and we got on with our studies. I joined the Viking High School Band as base drummer and really enjoyed it. That fall Air Cadets came into being so three days after that I was an air cadet. Our art teacher, Helen Towers was interested in music and started a glee club which I joined along with Arnold. Of course there was another attraction there. A pretty young girl, Eileen Child went there too. She was in my class and we became very close friends. She and her sister lived in a very small two room house and I went over there to do homework. As time went on they invited the cadets from Rodino to drop in after parade. Five cadets came in one night a week for parade. Ian Daniel took a shine to Gwen Child, Eileen's sister. A coupe of years later they were married.

The cadets needed uniforms so I arranged a cadet dance in Rodino hall as a fund raiser. This dance was held in mid October. I had completed my year in Viking and was back working on Billy's threshing crew. On the day of the dance it started to snow about noon. We had to shut down threshing. I had to go into Viking to pick up the girls and by the time we got back to the hall it was getting colder; in fact a blizzard was brewing. We had a huge crowd at the dance and raised enough money for the uniforms. We sure looked smart with our shiny shoes and polished brass.

The trip back to Viking was a disaster. The 1928 Chevrolet started OK but the temperature was now -20 F. and the wind was howling. We got about 4 miles from the hall and were going down a hill when the car slipped into the deep ruts. This took over the steering. At the bottom of the hill the car jumped out of the rut and I suddenly found I had no steering. The radius rod had been jarred out of place and the car went down a steep bank and into a slough. There was no way we could get it out. I went up to a house and asked the man if he would pull us out with his tractor. He said, "Not in this kind of weather!" and shut the door in my face. Fortunately a fellow came along in a Model T Ford and he gave us a lift to town. There were no floor boards in the back of that car and the girls got a bit of frost bite on their legs. Anyhow we got to their place and got warmed up at about 5:00AM. I phoned home and mother told me that Harry Johnston was going to be in Viking that day. We found him in the Viking Café and he took Ian and I home.

The next morning Alfred and I filled a cream can with hot water and wrapped it in blankets and set out with the team and sleigh. We had to chop the car loose from the ice and then hooked a logging chain on to the car. The horses could almost move it but lost their footing on the frozen road. As luck would have it, the truck hauling wood to the school, came along and it got the car back up on the road. We got the radius rod back in place and wired it on with a bit of wire from the fence. We poured the water into the radiator and it started with the first try. The next thing was to plow snow all the way back home. After quite a bit of shoveling I got the car home just as it was getting dark. We all survived the ordeal and carried on our regular routine.

Shortly after I went to school in Viking Mother discovered that she was pregnant. I don't think Father was very happy to hear about that. The baby was due at the end of February of 1942 and Mother would come to stay at the Cary's at that time to be close to the hospital. At the beginning of January Mother had labor pains and came to Viking. It was a false alarm but Doctor McBride suggested that she stay in town. On January 4th at 3:00 am we were awakened by Mother saying that it was time to go. Mr. Cary and I went out to start the Buick but, being -40 F it would not budge. There was neither ambulance nor taxi in Viking. He was the accountant for the Ford garage and had a key. We walked the six blocks and the only vehicle we could find the keys for was the hearse so we took it. We took Mother to the hospital in that vehicle, a comfortable Cadillac. The doctor told Mr. Cary and myself that we may as well go home because it would probably be the next day before anything happened so we went home and got a bit of sleep.

I went to school but couldn't get into my work for thinking about Mother. There was no word from the hospital until I got home and was told to get up to the hospital. Mother had given birth to a tiny little girl She was in an incubator and may not survive. The next afternoon I was called to the office. A nurse was there to see me. I dreaded what she might tell me. She told me that the baby was fine and handed me a list of baby things to get from the drug store. Father was away and so I would have to do the shopping. This was going to be fun because two of the girls in my class worked at the drug store after school. They were only too willing to help me with my purchases and equally willing to tell the rest of the class about the baby. I was called, Papa or Daddy" for a few days but it soon wore off. Mother and I discussed naming the little girl and decided on Fay Elizabeth. They had to stay in hospital for a week and then another week at Cary's so I got chances to hold, feed, and burp the tiny one. I even got to change her diapers. Alfred came in the car and took them home to the farm.

When Mother went home I was able to concentrate on my studies and other activities. Mr. Cary let me use his curling stones and broom and I joined the school curling club skipped by Ursula Webber. We did very well winning 2nd place in the finals. David Cary had joined the Fleet Air Arm shortly before I came to Viking. In fact I had taken over his room. Near the end of January a fateful telegram came. David had failed to return from a mission over France. A few days later another telegram confirmed that he had been killed in a low level strafing mission. This was the first experience for me to experience grieving as a result of the war.

The Cary's had four children. Bill was the oldest, followed by David, Sheila, and Patricia. Bill was attending University and the girls were at home. Sheila was in my class, a very studious type. Patricia was in grade five and did her best to get under my skin. Mrs. Cary taught piano lessons, played the Church organ, and was involved in many musical events. Mr. Cary had an excellent singing voice and was involved in many musical events as well. I was very fortunate to have such a good place to stay.

It was natural for me to go to Church every Sunday and I got to know Rev. Jones very well. One day he asked me if I had ever considered going into the ministry. We had a long discussion over it and at last I told him that there were many things I wanted to do in my life and I didn't think that I could give the dedication required of a minister. I continued to do odd jobs around the church and often gave thoughts about the ministry. This would indeed make Mother very happy. One evening I was at the church and Rev. Jones asked me if I would like to use his new car some time. I took him up on it and on a Saturday night loaded it up with some of my classmates and we went out to Lake Thomas for a wiener roast. On the way home a couple of the kids were bugging me; all in fun, and we wound up in the ditch. There were a couple of small scratches on the side of the car which I showed to him. He shrugged it off but he didn't offer me his car again.

A very good friend of mine, Bill Gillespie lived with his mother next door to the Cary's. Bill's ambition was to be a construction engineer and was making model aircraft in his spare time. This was right down my ally so I spent many hours over there. We specialized on gliders and even designed our own. There was a hook on the nose onto which we slipped a loop of a long string. We would run with it and when it reached a good height, the loop would slip off. On a hot summer day the craft would ride the air currents for along time. In fact, we labeled the craft with our address in case it flew out of the area. We even installed lights on the wing tips and wired them to a battery in the fuselage. Next we rigged up a small parachute and when the glider was released it also pulled a pin that let a trap door in the fuselage to open and the weighted parachute came out and floated to the ground. We even attached a battery and a light so that we could see where it landed after dark. Bill worked at his uncle's hardware store on Saturdays and brought home some shot gun shells. All the news on the radio was about the bombing in the war. We got some plaster of Paris and made a mould in the shape of a bomb, complete with fins. The detonator of the shell was faced forward and we placed a nail in the nose cone so that when the bomb landed the nail would strike the detonator and, Boom!! Now, because we didn't know exactly where it would land, we took cover in a ditch after we launched the glider. The first trial was a huge success. We got the loud bang we expected but not a big hole in the ground we thought might result. Anyhow it was good enough that we made a much larger mould so that we could make six bombs at a time. Mrs. Gillespie stared at the box and wanted to know what we were up to. Of course the answer was. "Nothing". One Saturday afternoon we went out to the big pasture and set about dropping bombs. Shortly a car drove up and the local Mounted policeman came to us and asked, "What are you boys up to"? We explained to him what it was all about and he replied, "This is all very ingenious boys but the farmer has complained that you are scaring the dickens out his cows and their milk production is suffering. Besides that it is in contravention of the law to carry on this sort of thing; especially in the town limits. Now pack up your stuff and I don't want to hear any more about bombs". That was the end of that.

It was now near the end of April and final exams were looming ahead. It was time to really concentrate on my studies. I got word that Father was coming home and would be arriving at Minburn at 3:00am on Saturday and it would be the first time he would see his new daughter. I was so anxious to be there for this event that I decided to walk the eighteen miles to the farm. On Friday right after school I rushed home to Cary's and against Mrs. Cary's advice I set out. The roads were half mud and half ice and snow. The going was very tough but I was determined and I arrived home at 6:00 pm. Mother was wondering how we would get to Minburn to get Father. I volunteered to drive the car. By this time the temperature had gone down and the mud firmed up so there should be no problem. We set out at 1:00 am and arrived in plenty of time to meet the train. I have never seen such a reunion before or since. Father was more than pleased to hold his new daughter and to see all of us again.

I had developed a very sore throat and Mrs. Tommy said that I would have to have my tonsils out. I hitched a ride to Kinsella with the mail man, taking the bicycle to ride the rest of the way, about 10 miles on the gravel highway to Viking.

An appointment had been set up with Dr. McBride and I went straight to the hospital. It was a very painful operation and I thought I was going to die. However I was back in school in three days.

On the 24th of May the school band was to perform at a neighboring community for their big sports day. I was also in a ball tournament that day. The band was to perform at predetermined times at the main concession area. After the first game I sought out Eileen who was also in the band and we were watching one of the sports events when all of a sudden we heard the band strike up on the other side of the field. We ran over there and slipped into our position. Relieving whoever had taken over for us. This did not go unnoticed by the band master Mr. Elliott who was also the principal of the school. The next piece was a lively march that was supposed to be culminated by a loud cymbal crash by me. At the appropriate time my fingers got tangled with thong of the beater and there was dead silence. Mr. Elliott's baton came at me like an arrow. I credit this event for a slightly lower mark in music than I had expected. At the end of June exams I returned to the farm and once again went to work for Billy Revill.

I continued to attend Air Cadet Parades and that summer we went to camp at Penhold, Alberta. This was a training base for the RAF under the Commonwealth Training Program. We were under their military command and treated as new recruits. This was the real thing. We took regular drill exercises a bit of Link Trainer. Learned to fold a parachute, and wore that same parachute in a familiarization flight in an Airspeed trainer plane. We even fired a browning machine gun and took some small arms training. My last parade was in October where I was awarded my discharge from the corps.

This was indeed a sad day for me but then I was looking forward to joining the RCAF as soon as I turned eighteen.

Mother told me that Father had been transferred to Vancouver and wanted Joyce and I to move out there to be near him. We were to go as soon as the harvest was done. At our last threshing job it began to snow, shutting down the threshing for the year. A couple of days later I hitched up to the wagon and went to pick up my bedroll from the bunk house. I pulled up to the fence and went in to get my bedroll. I heard an awful rumpus outside and when I came out the two horses were lying on the ground. Apparently one of them had a heart attack and was dead and lying across the other one's legs. With help of Fred Vandervaat and Debs Faulkner we got the horses untangled and the harness off the dead one. I borrowed a team from Fred and headed for home leading the other horse behind the wagon..

As I turned in at the gate my mind went over my life on the farm. I was looking for the last time at the old farm house, now showing its age. I would be saying goodbye to the barn, the animals, and to the fields where I had worked since I was a child. I would be saying goodbye to my Mother, my brothers, my dear old Grandmother, and to my sweet little sister Fay. As the wagon rumbled over the frozen ground some kernels of grain bounced on the floor of the rack. There was the wood pile and the frozen sheets clinging to the page wire fence. All of this stared at me as I drove a team of horses for the last time. What lay ahead of me in a new adventure of my life? In a letter from Father I was told that there was work in the ship yards building war ships or in the Boeing Plant building flying boats for the war effort. Joyce would have no trouble finding work either. Both of us were eager to be on our way.

We got our bags packed and Mother drove us to Viking to catch the 3:30 am train. Mother and Joyce took a room at the hotel so that Mother could see us off at the train station. I took a couple of hours to see Eileen and Gwen and we got to the station in plenty of time to say our goodbyes. Soon the train roared into the station blowing a huge puff of steam as it screeched to a stop. Joyce and I boarded the train and with a final wave we were off to Vancouver.

2001 "THE HOUSE"
    picture taken in July.2001

CANADIAN ARMY OVERSEAS

LEAVE PASS

Pass No. 4.   Date 9 Nov 45.

Pass No. 4.

No. KL239   Rank Pte   Name RAYMENT N.Y.

has permission to be absent from his unit from 0900 hrs. 12 Nov 45.

to 0900 hrs 15 Nov 45. for the purpose of proceeding to

PARIS, FRANCE.

Pass No. 4.

Regiment CIC

Army No. KL239

Rank Pte

Name RAYMENT N.Y.

Date from 0900 hrs 12Nov45

to 0900 hrs 15Nov45

PARIS
FRANCE.

Commanding

Station

Date

Orderly Room Stamp

9 NO. 1945
9 NOV. 1945
HQ. F1 CAMP
HQ. First Cdn. Army
(Unit Signature Stamp)

ENDORSEMENTS

Sec. 18(d)	R.T.O.—Station-Master—Local Police

INSTRUCTIONS

1. If you are travelling with free warrant have this pass stamped or endorsed in the space provided above by the R.T.O. station-master or local police at the place where you spend your leave. If you are unable to return to your unit due to interruption of transportation facilities have it endorsed to that effect by one of these officials.

2. Arms and equipment will not be checked at railway stations except during a wait-over between trains.

3. Carry this pass and your pay book (M.B.M.1) at all times while on leave.

4. **Illness on leave.**

   (a) Apply to the nearest unit of the Canadian Army, or

   (b) If none in the area, apply to the nearest unit of the British Army, request necessary treatment and that the O.C. communicate the facts to your unit. If unable to rejoin your unit before the end of your leave obtain a written report from the M.O. and hand to your C.O. on rejoining, or

   (c) If no military unit in the area, apply to a civilian doctor or the nearest Emergency Medical Service Hospital. Obtain a letter verifying the facts and send to your C.O. at once. If unable to rejoin your unit before the end of your leave obtain a certificate and hand to your C.O. on rejoining.

5. Turn this pass in on rejoining your unit.

4/13 CFA 24
40/P&S/1509
(In pads of 100)(5119)

1917   Albert Hugh Rayment and
       Helen Elizabeth Yeatman
       at the time of there
       engagement in London,

Grandma Yeatman with Helen Rayment, Fred and Joyce.
Albert Rayment's homestead shack in background

1955
Judy Bill
Donna & Lynda

Joyce, Alfred, Mother, Hugh, Fred
and Ken circa 1930

Ready for a buggy ride
1940

Tough going
Woodstock Ont. 1944

A brief leave of battle
Brussels 1944

Eiffel Tower, Paris 1946

Family gathering 1955
Ken, Hugh, Tom Fred
With Mom and Dad

The Rayment family
Tom, Hugh, Jouce, Fred,
Alfred, Mom, Dad, and Fay

Hugh & Elsie
Bill & Lynda
1049

1958 - Helen and Hugh Rayment

Hugh at book signing
2003

Chapter Six

Joyce and I had a wonderful trip on the train and as we approached Jasper we got our first glimpse of the Rocky Mountains. There was a twenty minute stop at Jasper so we got off the train to get a better view. It was a cold sunny morning making a perfect view for taking pictures of the pristine panorama of snow capped mountains. The rest of the trip to Vancouver was more and more spectacular. As we passed Mount Robson, this sentinel of the Rockies, we looked up and saw a white puffy cloud near the summit. The next spectacular landmark was the Fraser Canyon and then on to Vancouver.

Father met us at the station and we set out to walk the twelve blocks to where he lived. It wasn't long before we peeled off our winter coats to enjoy the summer like weather. Father had reserved a room for Joyce and he had a second bed brought to his room for me. Our address was 644 Bute Street near Staley Park. His plan was to move to a co-workers place as soon as Joyce and I had jobs and could support ourselves. When we had got moved in Father took us out for lunch at a famous waffle house on Robson Street. Because it was Saturday Father was off work and had time to show us around a bit. We strolled down to Stanley Park and what a change from Alberta. Everything was green and flowers were still in bloom. The smell of the ocean and the sounds of ships horns opened up a whole new life for us. All this was an experience I will never forget.

At this time we had to go to the Selective Service Office to get a card before we could even apply for a job. This was a wartime measure. Joyce had no problem getting a card but for me it was a different story. They told me that I should go back to the farm because there was such a shortage of farm workers. Many of the farm boys had left to join the forces, pressing even younger lads into the hard work of keeping the farms productive.

When I told Father about it he said that he would talk to his boss and see what could be done. The next day I got a call from Mr. Lawson, the District Inspector for Western Airways. He told me to go back to Selective Service and tell them who sent me. There was a position at Vancouver Airport and I should apply for it. The clerk at SSO reluctantly gave me my card and I went straight to the Airport. Firs I had to walk to the street car stop on Granville Street. This was a first for me and I stood on the sidewalk and expected the street car to stop but it kept going. A policeman told me I had to walk out to the loading pad and it would stop. I got on and asked the conductor how to get to the Airport. He gave me a transfer and told me to get off at 41st Avenue and get on a bus to Marpole. There I would have to buy another ticket on the Airport Bus. It took just over an hour to get there.

I went up to the Airport office and was greeted by Miss Willis, the secretary. There were others here waiting for an interview for the job. I was a bit nervous and was finally ushered in to see Mr. Templeton, the Airport Manager. He greeted me with a smile; probably because of my attire. I was wearing a pin-stripe suit that was sent in a parcel from England and wore a bowler hat. He motioned for me to sit down and asked me, "Well young man! What do you know about aircraft? I proudly produced my discharge certificate from Air Cadets and he stared at it for a moment and I blurted out, "I learn fast and only need to be shown what to do once". He looked back at the certificate and then at me and said, "Can you start tomorrow. Of course I answered in the affirmative. As I was leaving the office, Mr. Templeton said, "By the way, a pair of coveralls would be more appropriate than the suit and we will see you get a different hat. So this is how I got the job at the Airport.

Father was thrilled to hear the news and Joyce came in and said that she was going for an interview in the morning. My first shift was at 7:00 am the next morning and I probably got there at 6:00 and was ready for anything they wanted me to do. Finney McGar, the assistant manager, came in at 7:00 am and took me under his wing. The main runway was being extended and widened to take larger aircraft so the runway lights were out of service. Emergency lights, oil blow pots, had to be set out every night and then picked up, cleaned and refueled in the morning. So this was my first job. Next came refueling aircraft and we had to know what octane level of gas to put in each plane. We also checked the oil and then spin the prop to start the engine on small planes. The bigger planes were generally looked after by the ground crews of the airlines although we had to gas them up.

There was a seaplane base there as well. It was situated on the Fraser River and it was our duty to pull the float planes up to a ramp with a Ford tractor. Next we had to go to the back of the plane and fasten a restraining rope to the plane while the pilot taxied it down the ramp into the river. We also had to service these planes, including pulling them back up the ramp and down to the hanger. Shuffling aircraft around was an exacting job. There was no room for error. If so much as a scrape of a wing happened that aircraft had to go through an inspection by a competent inspector before it could be put back into service. I became very good at it and didn't have one mishap all the time I was there. There were many other tasks to do to keep the airport running smoothly.

Vancouver Airport was also shared by the RCAF, so it was under military guard 24 hour a day. The Boeing Aircraft Plant was also located on Sea Island next to the Airport. They were turning out a PBY aircraft every day and, as they were amphibian they could be test flown from either the main runways or on the river. Thousands of women worked at this plant and it was quite a sight to see all these girls in white coveralls coming and going.

The Air force had their own hanger and service facilities on the other side of the field so we didn't have anything to do for them other than see that the runways were serviceable. They were flying a variety of war planes and patrolled up and down the coast watching for enemy activity. There was a real threat from Japanese subs, and other means of invasion or bombing of the West Coast of America. All windows had to be blacked out every night, including civilian homes. The Army had gun emplacements all around the Airport as well as up and down the coast. We were truly on a wartime footing.

In the winter of 1942 there was a huge snowfall and we had to keep the runways serviceable. All runways had to be marked with lights at night and any obstruction had to have a red lantern placed on it. One night the fog rolled in and the City had not yet painted the yellow line down the center of the Airport road. Bob Scott, the field superintendent, showed up with some five gallon drums of yellow paint and some big paint brushes and two of us painted those stripes on the two miles of road. We had blisters on our hand by the time that job was done. During that same time there was a gale blowing in off the coast and we had to put the blow pots out on the runways.

Our panel truck was out of service so we used Bob Scott's new pickup. It was open so it would be difficult to light the pots in that wind. The fellow that was helping me suggested that we light them in the shed and then load them onto the truck. As I was driving out to the runway one of the pots upset starting a fire in the back. Some of the pots boiled over and we had an inferno in the truck. I made a very sharp turn and stepped on the gas. This threw most of the pots onto the runway. Drove as fast as I could right to where the fire trucks were parked. The fire crew was ready and turned the extinguishers on and the fire was doused in a few seconds. When Bob saw his truck he was furious and we spent the next day sanding the scorched paint off down to the metal. I was glad to get our own truck back.

I loved my job at the Airport. There was always something to do. During the time of the big snowstorm there was a emergency flight coming in. A Grumman Goose was bringing in a sick nurse from the north. I tore out to the end of the runway to set off special flares. As I was returning to base the landing lights suddenly were turned on and the Goose was right on my tail. I couldn't get off the runway because there were six foot snow banks on either side so I just tramped on the gas and hit the taxi way just as the plane zipped by. I met with the pilot in the tower shortly after the ordeal and he just laughed and said, "I saw your yellow truck and had just enough room to get by you. Sorry if I scared you"!   On another occasion a passenger on a CPA flight to Victoria went bezerk and Ian Duncanson had to do a quick turnaround and land at the dock. Luckily there was husky fellow on board and he prevented the guy from getting up to the cockpit. The two of us were able to get him out of the plane and I took him into custody and turned him over to the police.

It came time to change the tattered wind sock on top of a 30 foot tower. I got the job. I don't like heights but the job had to be done so up the tower I went. It was well supported by guy wires but any gust of wind made it very precarious. I got the old one loose and dropped it to the ground. As I was fastening the new one in place it popped open and scared the dickens out of me. I got down OK but was very glad to see the end of that day.

There was a Diesel operated power station that would kick in automatically if there were a power failure. It had to be tested every month to make sure it worked and this was another duty of mine. So it can be seen that there was plenty to do even when Vancouver Airport was relatively small. There were only three airlines working out of there along with a couple of charter outfits and the regular civilian flying clubs.

Passengers and crew of foreign aircraft were required to go through customs, show their flight plan, pay a landing fee, and, in some cases, show an airworthiness certificate. It was one of my jobs to greet the 1st officer and conduct him through these procedures. On one occasion a plane came in and I went to meet it. It was from the States and was a beat up old Stinson aircraft. There was an open barrel of gas behind the pilot's seat with a thief pump in it so that the pilot could manually refuel in flight. He had no flight plan and said that he was on a government mission to photograph timber areas in Northern B.C. I took him straight to customs and he was ordered to go directly back to the States and not to come back without prior permission from Canadian Customs. We never saw him again.

The night shift, 11:00pm to 7:00am was worked by a fellow by the name of Rolly. He liked that shift and worked it steady. When his holidays came up I volunteered to take over the shift. This job was very light because there was only a couple of night flights to attend to. To fill in the time the night man swept up the floors, emptied garbage cans and ash trays, and generally looked after anything else that came up. If there were any changes in field conditions a report had to be taken over to Canadian Airways who notified all stations. One night I got all my work done and went up to the tower for a game of bridge while waiting for the night flight of TCA from Calgary. Captain Ballentine reported in to the tower of his position over Hope. Gordy Miur responded and gave him the weather conditions and runway number for his approach. The next report from Flight 220 should have come about ten minutes later but there was no reply from an urgent request for position by Gordy. As it turned out Flight 220 Iced up on its decent and crashed into the peak of Mount Knight just outside of Hope. There were no survivors. I knew Capt. Ballentine well and joined all the staff in grieving for the popular and competent pilot. Two other pilots lost their lives flying from the seaplane base. They were CPA pilots flying Rapedes to the Island. Ian Duncanson went down as he ran into bad weather on approach to Victoria and Tommy Lorry met a similar fate going into Port Hardy. There were no survivors in either case. This was long before the jets came into use.

That summer I got word that Fred's Halifax bomber had been shot down in a bombing raid over Hanover, Germany. A short time later he was reported as a POW. This made me feel a bit nervous and perhaps a little guilty because I had exemption from military service because of my job. Other buddies of mine were joining up so I went to the RCAF recruiting station but was turned down. They said my night vision was not good enough to be a pilot and I didn't want anything else. I went to the Navy recruiting base and passed the medical alright but there was a three month waiting list. My eighteenth birthday was coming up and I would be getting a call from the Army so I took the bull by the horns and went to the Army recruiting office. There I was accepted immediately.

The next thing was to tell Father and Mr. Templeton what I had done. The easiest way was to go in uniform.   I went out to see Father first and when he saw me a very strange look came on his face and he said, "You didn't volunteer for active service did you"? When I told him that I had he spent about an hour telling me about the horrors of war. He knew I wouldn't back down even if I could. He later gave me a fine watch to bring me luck in battle.

When I entered M. Templeton's office he just stared at me in disbelief. Suddenly he broke out in a laugh and said, "I did the same damn thing in WW1. You make sure to come back here when it is all over".

Chapter Seven

On my first day in the Army I found out who was in charge. I had learned in Air Cadets about the different ranks, who to salute, and basic drill.

The new recruits were called out on parade by a sergeant and marched to the quartermaster's store where we were issued with fatigues. Next we piled into a truck and were taken to the freight yards. There we unloaded a boxcar of bunk beds. We had to assemble them in an empty hut and line them up, military style perfectly in line. Next, we were introduced to the mess line up with our issued mess tins and cutlery. With caps removed we passed huge vats of food that was ladled out into our mess tins and we moved on to long tables in the mess hall. I found the food to be very good and the servings were generous. We were soon to find out that finding fault with the food would only result in a spell of kitchen duty, i.e. scrubbing pots and pans or peeling vegetables, etc.

For the next week we were issued with our full kit which we had to put together. We were shown how to polish brass, shine shoes, make beds, and many other daily tasks that go with the life of a soldier. We were issued with rifles and a corporal instructed us in the care of weapons. After out vaccinations and inoculations we were ready to be shipped out to our first basic training camps.

We were loaded into TCV's and taken down to the train station where we boarded troop trains according to destination. I arrived in Wetaskiwin, Alberta boot camp in -20F temperature. We were marched about ten blocks to the camp and were glad to be inside and out of the cold. The double bunks were lined up; each wing of the H-hut accommodating 30 men. This would be six weeks of intensive infantry training. This is where we would be brought into shape for the future advanced infantry training at Currie Barracks in Calgary. Most of us were eighteen years old and for many it was their first trip out of the province of British Columbia. This was no camp for sissies. The training was tough and the discipline strict. Everything was spit and polish. All were given military hair cuts and we were kept under the watchful eyes of the military police when we were off duty. About this time I took up smoking and found that the wet canteen was a fun place to be. My pay was $1.40 a day so, in spite of the fact that cigarettes were 25 cents a pack of 25 and beer was 10 cents a glass, I had to be careful with my money. When I joined up I assigned $25.00 a month home to Mother and she put it into savings for me.

One night some of us were fooling around in the hut. I slipped on some water in the washroom and went headlong into a steam register. I got a gash over my right eye and the boys helped me over to the first aid hut. The Medical Officer was roused from his sleep to come over and stitch up the wound. A couple of nights later we were on a night exercise and I started to feel woozy and I fell down unconscious. Infection had set into the cut and I was hauled in to the camp hospital where I stayed for a week. It finally healed enough that I could return to duty. There was a court of enquiry into the whole affair but it was finally declared an accident and I heard no more about it.

At the end of the six weeks we had a final inspection and a trip through the gas chamber and then we were granted a weeks leave. I boarded the train to Edmonton and then transferred to the bus for Kinsella. Alfred picked me up and we drove to the farm. I was pretty proud of my uniform and, in fact, went to the Air cadet parade and gave a short report on what it was like to be in training camp. I visited with my friends including Eileen and found it a bit difficult to get on the train to return to camp.

As soon as we got back to camp we were marched to the station and boarded for Calgary. This was toughening up camp where they trained us for overseas service. We spent a lot of time out at Sarcee on the rifle range. There was a very cold snap and we went to the range. We had to fire our rifles with respirators on. They even released some tear gas to make it a little more realistic. The bayonet drill was cruel and at the end of the course we went on a 40 mile route march. It wasn't all marching either. Part of the way we had to run and some of it crawling in the ditch. We were in good shape and a buddy and I went to a dance that night. On the morning before final inspection I was called off parade to the administration build-ing. An Officer interviewed me and asked me if I ever got a message from the Department of National Defense. I told him that I got a call from the Navy but didn't think I could do anything about it. He asked me what I did with it. I told him that I tore it up and he said, "you never tear anything up from DND. He said that I could transfer if I wanted to but I declined because I would probably have to do boot camp again. He said, "While you are here I tell you that we have been watching you and can offer you a dispatcher's course". I replied, "If that is riding motor cycles I don't want any part of it". Then he as ked me if I would like to take a 3 inch mortar course which I jumped at. This was right down my ally and I was very good at it. We drove around Sarcee in Brengun carriers and had a whale of a time. I rarely had to fire more than one positioning round to get on target. This was a six week course and then we were shipped down to Woodstock, Ontario for a driver mechanics course.

This course consisted of driving all sorts of military vehicles in all sorts of conditions. We spent half days driving and the other half in the shops learning the mechanical part. The only disturbing part of the course was that there were ten of us who spoke English and about a thousand French Canadian fellows who were not signed up for voluntary service. We made up our minds to get along with them and we got through the course in fine style, I with top marks. On June 6th, 1944 the Colonel called us all out on parade. He announced that our troops had landed in Normandy. [D Day]

He pleaded with the conscripts to step forward and volunteer for active service. After all we were there to liberate their home land. There may have been three or four stepped forward. The course finished and we were shipped back to Calgary for overseas draft. We were outfitted with front line gear and given a two-week embarkation leave. I went out to Vancouver to see Dad for a few days and then took the train for the farm. I was home for five days and I got a telegram to return to Calgary. This time the farewells were not so easy. What made it harder was that there was a fellow [conscript] returning to his camp and his family was all at the train crying because he was doing *danger time* in Suffield. I was going overseas to fight in the front lines. No matter, I was on my way.

When I got back to Currie Barracks the Calgary Stampede was on and the overseas draft was included in the parade. We were dressed in all our overseas gear and felt pretty proud as we marched along. In a couple of locations we were booed. I guess some Calgarians were sick of the sight of soldiers. We sat around the barracks for a week and then were taken to board the troop train for Halifax.

We were allotted three to a double seat with all our equipment. Nobody complained about the cramped quarters. We were tough seasoned troops and were anxious to get overseas and into the fray. The trip across the prairies and across Ontario was uneventful until we reached the Province of Quebec. At one point the train stopped to take on water. Some of us got off to stretch our legs and some hoodlums came running down from the village throwing stones at us. We were hustled back on the train before the situation escalated. Later that day the train came to sudden halt. The tracks had been blown by saboteurs and we were held up until repairs were made.. We were glad to move into the Maritimes and eventually into Halifax. The train pulled right on the dock where our ship, the Empress of Scotland, was tied up. Thousands of troops boarded that ship and were expertly shown to their positions. Some were below decks and the open decks were fitted with bunks to accommodate 3 men each tier. These bunks were protected from the weather by heavy canvases. I occupied one of these bunks.

When I got my position on the ship I talked to a couple of sailors that were crew members. They told me that if I wanted a good trip to volunteer for gun crew. They pointed out the Officer to speak to and that is what I did. I was put on a regular watch and issued a heavy sea coat. I had to stand watch for four hours at a gun station. The duty was to watch for submarines or any suspicious looking objects out in the view from my station and report directly to the bridge if anything were sighted. My station was on a large naval gun on the upper deck of the ship and next to the bridge. If we sighted anything we were to get the gun ready for action and the regular navy boys would take over. Now for the good part!! When we got off shift we were escorted down to the galley and fed a hot meal. We didn't have to stand in line for anything.

The ship took a zigzag course across the Atlantic in six days. It could outrun any vessel and with the sonar system was relatively safe from enemy submarines and other war ships. I saw a light far out to sea and reported it to the bridge. The ship was immediately turned to avoid whatever it was. It caused a little excitement as the Navy boys scrambled to action stations and took over from me.

On the sixth morning I was on watch as the sun rose. I was in a perfect position to see the coast of Ireland as we sailed into Liverpool. I never saw such a wonderful sight. It was so green above a rugged coast line. We were unloaded at the Liverpool dock in a very orderly fashion. My section took turn and marched down the gang plank directly to a waiting train. Very quickly the train was off with the strange little toot of the locomotive. In a few hours we boarded trucks and were taken to Camp Norton not far from Nottingham in the midlands of England.

Our barracks consisted of open ended Nissan huts and we slept on wooden platforms with one blanket. This was to be the last toughening up course before going across the English Channel to the continent and into combat. Many of the boys became very somber and were busy writing letters home when off duty. The commando training was brutal but we knew that battle was near. The camp was situated on a big estate at the edge of Sherwood Forest. There were tourist signs indicating certain activities of Robin Hood. The Lord of the manor had a fish pond fed by a winding stream. Some of us decided that we wanted some fish. We threw a couple of hand grenades into the pool and stunned fish came to the surface and we were able to wade out and pick them up. We cooked them over a fire and really enjoyed them. We were not so joyous when the Colonel got wind of it and put us through Hell for a couple of days and nights.

That was the end of that caper.   We were there for a month before being on the move again.   This time it was to Aldershot not far from London. This is a huge camp with thousands of troops from many countries. It was an assembly point for movement of troops to the front. We were placed in cold barracks to await transport to an embarkation port. The place seemed to be crawling with Officers who picked every chance to give us a going over for deportment or untidy dress. Thank goodness we were only there for a couple of days. We were turned out for a medical on the parade square in the nude. An snotty English major stood on a box and gave us his farewell speech. He said, "You Canadians will soon be fighting a very clever enemy. I know you will bring honor to Canada and the British Empire. God speed and good luck"! Back in our barrack we prepared to move out dressed in full marching order. We climbed into trucks and were taken to the railway station, boarded a train, and were on our way. It was still dark when we arrived in Folkston, a channel port. We climbed a very steep hill to a camp on the top of the cliff. There were tents but they were all occupied so we had to be content to climb into slit trenches and tried to get some sleep in a wet drizzle.

In the morning we were free to go into the town with the warning that we must say nothing to the civilians with regard to our destination. A buddy of mine from boot camp and I were walking along the dock when an old salt [sailor] invited us aboard his fish boat. He gave us a drink from an oak keg. It was very thick and almost black. It went down very smoothly but must have been very, very strong. He said, "I don't expect you to tell me where you are going because I know damn well where you are going. He told us that he had lost a son on D-Day. As we left he wished us good luck and we started back up the hill. That rum was so strong that we did part way up the hill on our hands and knees.

The following morning we were paraded down the hill to the dock and we boarded a landing craft and moved off into a very choppy channel. The water was washing over the deck and we were ordered below. That boat was being tossed about like a cork. Some of the guys were sea sick and throwing up. It was a terrible stench but I didn't get sick. Suddenly the sea calmed and we thought we were in France. We disembarked into a large mess hall and were fed rice pudding with raisins plus a mug of tea. The boat had to turn back and we were in Dover. In the morning we boarded the craft again and the channel was smooth as a plate. It was not long before we could see the coast of France. As we approached shore we could see the devastation caused by the invasion. Buildings were ravaged, trees were mashed and the power lines hung in disarray. There was a haze of smoke over the whole area and we could hear the sounds of guns as Caen was being battered by our artillery. We came ashore in a dry landing on a dock that had been towed across the channel and assembled by the engineers at Arromanches. This was an idea conceived by Winston Churchill. We were marched up a corduroy road and directed by a provost where to dig in for the night. We knew that battle was not far off and slept a fitful sleep. In the morning we were awakened by a call for breakfast.

After a hearty meal we climbed into trucks headed for the front. We were to join the Calgary Highlanders by nightfall. On the way our convoy was halted and three trucks were rerouted up another road. Just as it was getting dark we came under shell fire and bailed out into the ditch. There were dead bodies of German and Canadian soldiers along the roadside. Through the gloom a troop of soldier carrying assault boats came by. We were ordered to fall in with them. We were to assault across the Leopold Canal. This was a double channel canal to afford two way-traffic for the barges transporting goods in that part of Belgium. When we got to the bank of the canal we got in the boats and paddled across the first stretch and then had to drag the boats over a very rough segment. Some of the boats got ripped on the rocks and were rendered useless. We came under shell and small arms fire but managed to reach the far bank. I didn't really know what was going on but learned very quickly to keep my head down. Our officer ordered us to advance and we moved up to a row of trees. The fire was devastating and many of our troops were killed or wounded. It had been anticipated that resistance would be light but a troop of German Panzer tanks had not been detected. The night wore on and the tanks move in for the kill. By noon we were nearly out of ammunition and it became certain that we could not proceed or even hold the beachhead. We were ordered to get back across the canal as best we could. Most of the boats were destroyed and many of us had to jump in and swim. I saw German prisoners helping our wounded into boats but I don't really remember how I got back.

The first thing I remember was running down a cobble stone road in my bare feet and there was a shell coming in. A sergeant and I ducked into a building and took cover under a counter. The shell hit the building and we emerged covered with white powder from the plaster. We looked up at a shelf still lined with bottles of booze. We each grabbed one and took off down the road. A Brengun carrier came by and I recognized one of my buddies in it and I jumped on and we proceeded about a mile down the road. The remains of the assault troops were reforming here. My Buddy, Emil Liska, sat under an apple tree and we killed that bottle of booze.

The sergeant major was trying to get a count of the survivors and when he called out for 13 platoon I answered. There was only one other fellow that got back unwounded. The rest were either killed or taken prisoner. To this point I didn't know what Regiment I was with so I asked one of the guys and he told me that it was the Algonquin Regiment of the 4th Armored Division. This was a very rude inoculation to battle. However this is war and anything can happen. We were pulled back for regrouping and reinforcement. The Colonel congratulated us for a courageous battle and announced that our attack had pulled German troops from another front making an assault by another regiment a resounding success. It was here that I was able to write letters home. I told them that I was OK but could give no more information on account of tight security. All mail was censored.

After this we drove the Germans out of several small towns and took hundreds of prisoners, sustaining very few casualties in our advance toward the Dutch border. The last place in Belgium was Assenede, a small city but the Germans had it well fortified. It was a beautiful sunny day. Birds were in the air; a sight rarely seen near the battle field. We heard a steady drone and looking up we could see hundreds of bombers, some towing gliders and they were headed East. This was the paratroop attack on Arnhem in Holland. We waved and hoped that this may be the end of the war. Alas, the Germans had been tipped off and were ready for them. It was a total failure with the loss of thousands of lives.

As we advanced on Assenede the guns opened up and we bailed off the tanks and advanced along a deep ditch by the road. The Germans had cut down some of the big trees that lined most of the roads there. This held up the tanks but the infantry moved on. As we were entering the town I found myself in a pig yard surrounded by a stone fence. Baby pigs were running around terrified by gunfire from a sniper in a Church steeple. I threw myself behind a pig trough for cover. One of the piglets got hit by a bullet and was squealing very loudly. The sow was locked in a pen at the far end of the yard. I noticed the big wooden door of the pen shaking violently and suddenly the door flew open and the big sow came charging out. She was headed straight toward me and I didn't know whether to make a run for it under fire or take my chances with the sow. Just as she was nearing me one of the little ones squealed down near the pen and she wheeled around to go to the aid of her baby. I jumped up and ran for the stone wall and was over it in a flash. I found my buddies in a ditch and we continued our advance. The Germans had placed a rail car across the road at the railway crossing and the engineers moved up with a bulldozer and pushed it out of the way so that our tanks could advance. We got well into the town and started clearing houses of enemy troops. One of the guys tossed a hand grenade at an upstairs window but missed. It came down at our feet and we didn't wait to clear that house before crowding in the door. The grenade exploded just as we were in to safety. Cpl Reinhart and I were standing in the hallway and a burst of enemy machinegun fire slashed through the wall just missing us. As we were leaving I saw a stream of blood running down the wall and went upstairs to investigate. A man had been struck by a large piece of shrapnel which had severed his head. I rushed downstairs and was about to leave the house when I saw a German soldier throw a potato masher in through the window. I threw myself to the floor and screamed out. There was a terrible blast that left me without hearing for three days. I didn't have a scratch on me and Cpl Reinhart pulled me out of there. When I regained consciousness the platoon was lined up with the tanks to make a final assault. I told the tank commander about the sniper in the Church steeple. The tank moved up to the crossroad and the turret swung around and up and boom! There was no more steeple on the Church and no more sniper. We moved through the streets with the tanks and at midnight the town was ours. My platoon was invited into a home and there was a very large Belgian woman working over big black pot on the stove. She had made a big pot of rabbit stew and served each of us a bowl of this delicious treat. Her husband brought up a bottle of brandy and after a bit of a celebration we fell asleep on the floor. I mark that as the best meal I had during the war. In the morning we were treated to some bread and jam and very strong coffee.

We joined the other members of the platoon in a dull cold morning. They were gathered in front of a building that the Germans used as a storehouse. There were piles of uniforms and other gear used by their men. One of the fellows came out with a box of fine cigars intended for German Officers. Some of us lit up and slipped into German greatcoats. We were soon ordered to take them off with the promise that our coats would be brought up.

Now it was time to press on after the enemy. Along with tanks from the South Alberta Regiment we proceeded toward the Dutch border. We cleared several small towns and villages including Phillipine Station and the town of Phillipine, and then on to Isabella. The battle here was very fierce as we confronted by S/S and Hitler Youth troops. They fought tenaciously because they were told that Canadians did not take prisoners. Many fought to the finish. As our casualty list grew the weather continued to get colder. And it rained most of the time. When we dug a slit trench it would half fill with water making it hard to find suitable cover. Houses were not a good choice because they were the target for German artillery. With all credit due to the boys in Italy and those that landed on D-Day this was some of the fiercest fighting of the war and certainly as miserable. The Germans were well entrenched in the dikes and were even fortified in concrete bunkers. All roads in this area were sewn with land mines and many articles in the houses were booby trapped. Fine tripwires could set off a mine anywhere. We had tanks equipped with a boom and a drum that rotated with lengths of chain attached. The chains would beat the ground ahead of the tank, detonating mines harmlessly ahead of the tank. The German 88 gun mounted on their tanks was a deadly weapon because its missile traveled faster than the speed of sound and we could not hear it coming. It would penetrate six inches of armor and fill a tank with molten metal. The crew would be lucky to survive and would be badly burned. We had an anti-tank device, the PIAT. It was carried by the infantry and its projectile would penetrate German armor releasing a fireball in the interior of the tank. This weapon had to be fired at close range and dead on the side of the tank. The Germans also had an artillery piece that fired multiple shells in quick succession and could blanket an area with devastating effect. We called it the moaning Minnie because of the sound of the approaching shells. Both sides had hand grenades that were carried by the infantry. Our 36 grenade was a deadly weapon used at close quarters. Our artillery had long and short range guns to match the firepower of the enemy.

We moved into position in an area known as the Breskens Pocket. We were stalled here for a month in the dikes. It was cold and miserable and we were holding an area behind a high dike. We went on frequent patrols trying to establish the strength of the German forces. One night we were preparing to cross a stream, hoping to bring back a prisoner for interrogation. I was detailed to carry a flame thrower. It was a devastating weapon and also made a first grade target in the dark when it was fired. Just as I was strapping it on my back a jeep came up and my name was called. I was up for leave of battle and would be away from the front for 12 hours. I was in that jeep in a flash and taken back to headquarters where about a dozen of us were loaded into a TCV and taken to Brussels. The first stop was a public bathhouse where we had a wonderful hot shower. We were issued with new clothes and then to a local barber shop where we were groomed to make us feel human again. Next to the barber shop was a photo shop and I went in and had a picture taken and sent home to Dad. He was dabbling in photography and made many copies of that picture. Now was the time for some fun. There was a bar and some very pretty girls to entertain us. We forgot the horrors of war for a short time as we danced the night away. At a designated time we had to be back at the pick-up point. Failure to be there could cancel all future leaves so we were all there to to return to the wet and the cold and the bullets.

When we got back we were given the new recruit treatment because of our clean uniforms. That didn't last long as we slid into our muddy holes and others got their turn for

LOB. The fellow that took over the flame thrower had the palm of his hand blown out with a piece of shrapnel. At least he was out of the war.

One night we were relieved by a British unit and were taken back for a few days of rest. We were bunked down in an abandoned convent. This was heaven indeed even though it was not heated and we slept on wooden floors. The following day we were cleaning our weapons and writing letters home. One of the fellows was cleaning his Brengun. He was on the verge of a nervous breakdown. He should have been evacuated for treatment but like many of us had to carry on. In his nervous state he cleared the gun with a full mag in place. The gun fired a burst and a chap across the room was fatally injured. It was a very sad funeral service performed by our padre. The fellow that fired the gun went completely berserk and was immediately evacuated. Things like this happen in war.

From here we took over a position held by the Black Watch. This town had exchanged hands with the enemy three times. It was not a good prospect for us. My buddy, Tinning, and I took over a trench in front of a hedge. We were on 50% stand-to which meant one of us had to be awake at all times. Thank goodness the weather was a little warmer and it was dry. We got settled in and I took my turn to snooze. All of a sudden there was a terrible racket. Unknown to us there was a Bofor gun on the other side of the hedge. It is an anti-aircraft gun but in this case was being used in a ground role. It fired five rounds in quick succession over our heads. That was a rude awakening along with the stench of cordite and smoke.

The next night the Germans sent a patrol to our position. We were able to fight them off with hand grenades and small arms fire and we suffered no casualties but they were wiped out.. A group of Belgian volunteers came up and wanted to help us out. Our officer sent them to take over the next street. In the morning I went over to see how they were making out. There were none to be found and on enquiry I was told that one of them had taken a bullet between his eyes and the rest left to arrange a funeral for him. We were lucky because they had left an open flank that the Germans could easily have taken advantage of.

After a week in that Hell-hole we were again relieved and moved out to another sector. As we advanced to a town called Ertvelt riding on the top of tanks we were confronted by a German Panzer tank. It let blast with the 88mm gun, knocking out two of our Sherman tanks. The tank I was on got a hit in front of the turret. I was on my way to the ditch and my rifle got blown to bits but I wasn't hit. The Panzer was dealt with by the boys in the South Alberta Regiment. We took The town and stayed there overnight. Street cars were still working and some of us got permission to go into town and find a bar. The only effect the beer seemed to have was to get our waterworks flushed out.

Our next advance was to and take the city of Bergen-op-Zoom in Holland. It was heavily fortified and we looked forward to a tough battle. We formed up in a bush beside the main road and got our equipment in shape for the following day. In the morning I was not feeling good and was shaking uncontrollably. I felt totally spent and when they suggested evacuating me I broke down completely. This was known as battle fatigue. They loaded me into a jeep ambulance and as it drove away I broke into tears. It was a terrible feeling that I was deserting my buddies when I knew they were short hand-ed.

I was admitted to a field hospital and the medical officer told me, "You won't be seeing front line service again. They put me to bed and I didn't wake up for three days. I don't remember any particular treatment other than sleep. Casualties were coming in from the battle for Bergen-op-Zoom and I felt a degree of guilt that I wasn't with them in the attack. However it did feel pretty good between white sheets and meals brought to my bed. After a week and, in spite of the fact that I still felt rotten, I was discharged and taken to a reinforcement base on Ghent, Belgium. There were hundreds of Canadian troops here recovering from wounds and others who had been transferred from the Air force and Navy, and other non-combat personnel because of the shortage of reinforcements for the infantry. I had a warm place to sleep albeit on a wooden floor with one blanket.

We were called out on parade each morning and some were placed on draft back to the front and others were selected to take infantry training. One morning I went on parade and I recognized the very familiar voice of my platoon sergeant. Sergeant Eaton had been wounded and was here to get his strength back and was assigned to give some of the training. I broke ranks and went up to him and said. "I don't really have to go through this do I"? He gave me a warm welcome and said; "Why don't you go into town and get drunk"? A fellow from the Black Watch and I did just that. In fact we stayed in town for three days. We were walking down a street and noticed a strong smell of fresh baked bread. We traced it to a bakery that had been taken over by the Canadian Army to supply bread for the troops. There was a chain link fence around the place but we found a hole and crept in to see if we could get some of that bread. We found an open window and looked in. There were shelves of fresh baked bread and bags piled up in a room by the stoves. This made a fine bed and we had plenty to eat. We sneaked out of there before the cooks came on duty. This is where we slept for three nights. I suggested to my buddy that we had better get back to barracks before the military police got us. It was a good decision because when we went on parade Sergeant Eaton called out my name. I was up for draft and was soon on my way. This time I was posted to the 2nd Canadian Road Construction Company of the Royal Canadian Engineers. I was placed on general duty which meant that I had practically nothing to do. I was billeted in a vacant house with no heat but I had three blankets on a real bed. We were in the town of Liege in Belgium not far from the Dutch border. This was the big offensive by the Germans threw the Americans back and almost cut off the Canadian forces in Holland. It was known as the battle of the bulge. Liege was a pivotal point of this attack and the Germans dropped some paratroops in this area to disrupt our communications. I was sent out in an armored car to search for them and bring them in. They didn't argue with the armored car and, in fact, seemed glad to get out of the war.

On Christmas Eave some German dive bombers came over and strafed the main street. I hid under a big oak table but only the house next door was hit by a bomb. The weather closed in and all air activity ceased for the time being. One day I saw a little boy with his sister standing at the curb. Our trucks were hauling coal somewhere and as they turned the corner some pieces of coal would fall off and the children would dash out and pick it up and scurry off with it. The next day I went over to them and the little boy took me by the finger and led me to the back porch of a house. A family of five was huddled around a tiny fire in a small oil drum. They were Dutch and had escaped into Belgium in the night. There was the grandmother, the mother, the two children that took me there, and a little baby, her tiny face covered in sores.

The mother could speak some English and she told me that the Gestapo had come to their house and shot the father because he had a radio. The town officials had given this dreadful place to stay with a very meager food allowance. I quickly got some cans of food from our kitchen and then went to City Hall and confronted city officials and ordered them to get that family in a house and a supply of milk for the baby. They were moved that day to a heated house and milk was supplied. It was amazing to see the sores on the little one's face heal in the next few days. I visited them every day and now often wonder what came of them.

I was still not well and on New Year's evening I went to bed early. When I awoke in the morning I had a terrible pain in my chest. A Corporal came to inspect the quarters and saw my distress. He got me down to the first aid post and the medical officer ordered up the stomach pump. He said, "Another case of too much to drink"! The Corporal suggested taking my temperature. It was 105 F. degrees. They quickly summoned the ambulance and I had a very rough ride to a British hospital where I lost consciousness. I lay there for three days with a pretty Scottish nurse looking after me. She stayed at my bedside for all that time. When I came to she said, "You are a sick laddie Canada". The medical officer put me on Sulfur medication and I was allergic to it so He said, "We will have to try the new miracle drug penicillin and so I was getting a shot in the bum every four hours. The nurse told me that he had said that I would be a job for the burial party in the morning. She was determined to keep me alive. She changed my sheet as I soaked them with sweat. Five days later I moved to another British hospital in Antwerp in an ambulance train. When we got there it was cold and snowing. We were placed on stretchers and unloaded on a large patio at the hospital. I had just one blanket over me and had to wait about an hour for my turn to be admitted. By this time the pain in my chest had returned and my temperature was up again. Once again I fell into a coma and when I came to the Matron told me that I had a relapse. She also told me to eat plenty because my weight had dropped to 89 pounds. Needless to say I felt very weak and lysergic.

About ten days after arriving there a German V-1 bomb landed near the hospital and blew in all the windows. I awoke in terror with glass all over my bed. I didn't have a scratch on me. We were evacuated from ther to St Omer where I slowly recuperated. In this hospital the matron took a liking to me and scrounged me some canned peaches. She was a strict old gal and one day there was to be an inspection by a senior medical officer and she told all of us in the ward to stand at attention when he came. I told her that I didn't think I could get out of bed and she retorted, "Then lie to attention soldier"!.

A month later I was transferred to a Canadian hospital. Here the medical officer didn't come around for three days and I received no medication. I was awakened by the Padre and he said, " I am sorry to wake you up but I just couldn't leave without talking to you". He told me about a young Canadian soldier who got leave to England and went to stay with his war bride. When he got back to his unit he came down with venereal disease and he didn't know whether he had taken it to her or if she had contracted it and gave it to him. I asked him, " what has this got to do with me"? He told me that I was in the venereal disease ward and he naturally thought that was why I was there. He got me moved out of there right away and I got back on to my medication. Captain White was my medical officer and at our first meeting he suggested that I should be at the front rather than taking up a bed in hospital. He said,

"You will be out of here tomorrow". I told him that I didn't think I could walk. He said, "You will get up today and go out tomorrow". They brought me hospital blues and a nurse got me on my feet. It was hopeless. I had to hold on to the bed or fall on the floor.

That night a senior officer came to inspect. When he came to my bedside he said, "This fellow doesn't look very good." Captain White said, "He is going out tomorrow Sir". The major asked to see my chart and when he read it he said, "This lad won't be going anywhere until he gets some meat on his bones". So it was that I stayed there for two more weeks and then transferred to a convalescent hospital near Dieppe, a city that was still in the hands of the Germans. We could hear the gunfire from there.

Here I was able to do a bit of walking and gained some strength. The medical officer there was much more sympathetic and he eased me into a bit of marching. I was issued with a British uniform and was told that there were no Canadian uniforms available. One Sunday I went into the village and saw British soldiers swaggering around in Canadian uniforms. They were even trying to talk like Canadians to impress the girls. I asked to see the Padre and it turned out to be the same one I had seen before. Before the sun set that day I had a full issue of Canadian kit including a Canadian uniform.

Finally, on April 10th I was discharged from hospital and once more I found myself at the reinforcement base in Ghent. I still didn't feel very strong but was glad to be on the move. After a few days I was transferred to Nijmegen in Holland. By this time the end of the war was in sight. The Russian forces were speeding westward and the western allies were across the Rhine and moving in to the heartland of Germany. We were in range of enemy guns but they were saving ammunition for the final assault. I was in a comfortable billet in a Dutch East India Camp that had been given over to the Canadian Army.

I was assigned to transport and was driving our officers around in a jeep. There was an education office there and I enrolled in a correspondence course, Principles of Radio. Sgt. Major Weeks was in charge of the program and I volunteered to help him out. I met some of the officers and one day was asked if I would like to run the officers' bar. This was a very good job and I enjoyed it. A young girl, Rea Sanders worked in the camp and I met her at a camp dance. We went for a walk one Sunday and I told her I would like to meet her family. She said that her father did not like soldiers; not surprising because they lived just outside the camp and he saw them everyday. Somehow the subject of music came up and I told her I could play the piano. I did know a couple of pieces my grandmother had taught me. The next Sunday Ria told me that her father wanted to meet me and I was invited to dinner. Her father was an accomplished pianist and when I got there the music was all set out for me; Beethoven I think. When I saw this I froze. I was ushered to the piano by Mr. Sanders. He didn't speak English and I tried to explain that I couldn't play anything like that but he insisted, through Ria's interpretation, and so I rattled off, "The March of the Wooden Soldiers" Mr. Sanders glared at me and then suddenly a big smile crossed his face and he welcomed me into his home.

Ria had two little brothers and I had a great time playing with them as I became a regular visitor there. There was no romance between Rea and I; just a good friendship and besides it gave me some family life. One day Mr. Sanders brother was there visiting from Bloomendaal, a costal town near Amsterdam. He was an accountant at the Royal Palace and he invited me to come up on my next leave. I accepted the invitation and on the next weekend I caught the leave truck to Amsterdam. I was met by my host and we caught the train to Bloomendaal. Mr. Sanders had been a leader in the Dutch underground and he showed me his secret radio room in the cellar. There was still dancing in the streets every night and I joined in, escorting his beautiful daughter. Mrs. Sanders served up a huge meal of boiled mangols, normally used as cattle feed. I had brought some canned goods with me and the family was overjoyed to share it in the meals. It must be understood that there was still very little food in Holland. Over a million people had starved to death during the German occupation. Mr. Sanders told me of a family that had boild up some old shoes for soup stock and had mixed grass with it to survive.

Shortly after I returned to Nijmegen I was transferred to another part of town as the commanding officer's driver.

On one occasion I drove him to Brussels to take his dog to the war dog training center where there was a vet. Apparently Capt. Cardwell's dog was sick but I think it was an excuse to go there because he stayed with a lovely lady. I was billeted in a very nice hotel and had the use of the jeep when the captain didn't need my services. On day I was downtown for a few drinks and took the rotor out of the distributor as a precaution against theft. When I came out two Canadian soldiers had the hood up on the jeep and were trying to get it going. I noticed that they were wearing Algonquin shoulder flashes. I took them to my room and we shared a bottle of rum. The Regiment was on the way to England and repatriation. They were camped at a village not far from Brussels. I drove them there and a big party was underway. It was a good opportunity to say farewell to my old comrades.

I got leave to England when I got back to Nijmegen and caught the train to Calais and the ferry to Dover. My first stop was London. I went to Victoria Station and phoned Mother's cousin in Limpsfield, Surry to see if I could come down to visit. She said, "Oh please do. Fred just phoned and is on his way here. This was the first news I had of him since he was a prisoner of war in Germany. There he was catching the same train. And what a reunion. We were given a very nice guest room at Barb and Alleyn's place. Fred and I spent the next three days comparing notes and then Fred suggested that we visit the Hoskin's Arms, a pub in the village. This was the start of many visits to many pubs from one end of England to the other. Fred had a girl friend in Nottingham so we went up there and one evening we went to a dance. I met a very nice girl, Marie Swan who was in the ATS [British Woman's Army] I rented a boat and took her for a row on the river Trent and we had a great time while we were there. She had to go back to her camp and Fred and I continued on our spree. Fred was very thin because of the starvation diet when he was in the POW camp. He was also in the forced march across Germany in the winter of 1945. The column of prisoners was mistaken for Germans by the RAF and they strafed them and some were killed. Fred got a piece of shrapnel in his cheek but otherwise survived the brutal march. . There had been only 400 survivors out of 800 starting the march. Many froze to death and others just were too weak and died on the road.

They were liberated by the British Army and sent to a Canadian air base for transport to England. They were loaded into Lancaster bombers for the flight to England and on take-off the plane Fred was in crashed and caught fire. Miraculously they all escaped unhurt and he got to an RCAF camp in England. We had a marvelous time together and often talk about it.

On my return to Nijmegen I continued with my duties. The Padre asked me to drive him up to Denmark. I told him that I had to get the brakes on the jeep fixed before we could leave. I took the jeep to a British workshop and told them I was in a hurry because the Padre wanted to leave as soon as possible. After many phone calls I was finally told it was ready and I went to pick it up. It was sitting in the doorway of the shop. Just as I got there it was tea time and all the Limeys grabbed their mugs and disappeared into the back of the shop. However a Sergeant shouted out, "Take it away Canada"! I started out and at the end of the building I turned right. There was a railway crossing here. I drove over it many times and if there were a train coming a heavey barrier was down. It was operated by a man in a booth over the crossroad. This time the barrier was up so I proceeded. Through the corner of my Eye I saw a freight train barreling down on me. I had plenty of time to stop but when I applied the brakes there was nothing there. I turned hard to the right in an attempt to get off the tracks but the train caught the jeep and deposited it 100 yards up the track. The jeep was nosed into the bank and, with its wheels still spinning, I managed to crawl out with only a bad bump on my hip.

I got another jeep and drove up to the waiting Padre. I started a check of the vehicle which was a mandatory procedure before starting on a trip. The Padre told me not to bother with that so we got under way. As we approached Arnhem the jeep started acting up and stalled. Smoke was pouring out of it and the engine wouldn't budge. Fortunately there was a Canadian supply depot a few hundred yards from where we were stopped. I got the jeep toed in and they found that there had been no water in the radiator and the engine had overheated and seized. I asked the seargent how long it would take to put anew engine in the jeep. He just laughed and said, "Forget it!

There is a lot of red tape for that". I pulled a bottle of booze out of my kit and he said, "Give me an hour". That was that and we were soon on our way.

There was a lot of hullabaloo about the train incident but the engine trouble never came to light. I had to interview the train engineer and he told me the signal man had fallen asleep on the job and had been fired on the spot. Finally the incident was declared an accident and I was exonerated from any blame and I continued with my duties.

One morning I was crossing the lawn and I noticed an army caravan which is an officer's mobile quarters, parked nearby. A bald headed man stuck his head out of the door and called me over. It was Colonel Dixon and he asked me if I would bring him a basin of hot water. I got him the water from the kitchen and took it to him. He invited me in and we had a good talk. He had been a professional wrestler in Regina when he was younger. He came up through the ranks during a long military career and was now a lieutenant colonel. He was waiting for notice to retire. As I left he asked me if I would bring him hot water every morning.

About a month later Colonel Dixon asked me to drive him to Appeldoorn, Canadian headquarters in Holland. On the way he asked me how I would like to be his driver in Paris. He was taking over as Commanding Officer of the Canadian Leave Center there. I told him that I was pretty happy in Nijmegen but would think about it. He told me that this camp was going to be closed down shortly and I would probably be sent to the Occupation in Germany. He said, "If you come with me you will be on the boat for home in six months". I said, "I'll come with you", with a large grin on my face. Getting home was my top priority.

A week later I was on my way driving a luxury Packard staff car. We arrived in Paris late one night and were escorted to the Hotel Westminster by a Sergeant in a jeep. We got the colonel's gear moved into the hotel and Colonel Dixon asked the Sergeant, "Where will my driver be staying"? The Sergeant replied, " At the Quay Dorsey on the other side of the Seine. The Colonel retorted, "What's wrong with that room across the hall"? The Sergeant said that it was reserved for officers and the Colonel replied, "Put him in there. I want to know where he is when I want him". He was the commanding officer and what he said went so here was I in the lap of luxury. I could use the car if I wanted to but rarely did. As a matter of fact the officers usually used taxi cabs. Colonel Dixon kept me busy running errands for him. My room had a fireplace and a private bathroom. My bed was made up by a maid every day and was cleaned regularly. This was heaven indeed. I took in ironing for the officers and the other ranks there, giving me a few francs to spend. I kept the colonel's booze supply up by selling cigarettes on the black market as everybody else did. The Metro system in Paris was a wonderful way to get around. There were dances arranged by the leave center and girls came from the university and the famous girls finishing school to entertain the troops on leave. We were not supposed to date these girls but my buddy Pat Chaison and I got to know a few of them and did date them in our leisure time. I met a very nice girl who had very wealthy parents. They spent a lot of time at their seaside villa and had a penthouse apartment in Paris. The girl's name was Simone Poupinelle and she was attending the University of Versailles. She showed me around Paris and explained many of the historic places to me. We went to the Louvre and to the famous opera. When I went to visit her I was greeted by the butler. He would say, "Attende sil vous plaise", and then announce me in the drawing room to Denise, "Entree le Monsieur Raymond"! I never got over this elegant introduction. One Sunday Denise and I went riding at a local riding school and then canoeing on Lac Beloyne. We went to the Paris Zoo and Tuillery gardens and many other famous sights in that beautiful city.

The Americans had taken over the Eiffel Tower as a radio transmitting medium and they broadcast all the favorite songs of the time. I had a local radio technician make me a radio that was a bit scratchy but wonderful to listen to, "Its Midnight in Paris", with the likes of Bing Crosby and Bob Hope. Pat and I had befriended a Paris policeman and his wife and they invited us to dinner at his mother's place in Versailles. Now this was an elegant mansion. We sat down to supper at 7:00 pm and were still there after some of the family got back from midnight mass. The courses and the wine kept coming and when we finally got up from the table we went into a ballroom and musicians provided music for a wonderful dance. We were shown to luxurious guest rooms and were called in time to have breakfast and catch an early train back to Paris. We enjoyed a Christmas dinner put on by the Army and traditionally served by the officers.

Shortly after Christmas Colonel Dixon told me that he was going home for discharge and retirement. This was a sad day for me indeed because I was transferred to the hotel across the river and general duty. I took a job on the telephone switchboard not realizing that most of the calls were in French. By this time I was fairly fluent in French and made out fairly well.

One day I was walking down Rue de la Paixe and I met one of the officers. They had moved from the Hotel Westminster to an estate on Avenue Kleber. They were happy there because they were on Canadian rations rather than the scant British rations. I asked the officer if there were any jobs there and he told me that they needed a bar steward. I told him that I had expeience in Holland and he invited me to apply for the job. I went there immediately and was transferred there the next day. I was given a very nice room over the garage and introduced to the kitchen and bar staff. They were civilians and willing to show me the ropes of my new job. I was in charge of the bar and all operations regarding meals for the officers. I could have received a promotion to full Corporal but, for some stupid reason, preferred to remain a private. I also got to drive the Packard and sometimes went over to the Canadian Embassy to pick up General and Madame Vanier and bring them over to the Officers' Mess. On one occasion I took Madame Vanier on a shopping trip. She was a very gracious lady and was very interested in talking about life in Canada.

The Major asked me if I could get some decent meat in the mess. I told him I would try but I would need a jeep and some good stuff to barter with. I was provided with a jeep, a driver and plenty of cigarettes. He even gave me a brand new pair of Gestapo boots. Away we went to a village not far from Paris. We went to a café and ordered a meal of chicken. When it came to the table I asked the chef "Is this roast cat"? He denied it but when I asked him where I could get some beef he directed us to a farm a little way from there. I asked the farmer and he said he didn't have any beef. I showed him the cigarettes and the chocolate bars but it was still no. When I showed him the boots he said, "Come with me", and led us to a concealed well in the bush. Having unreported meat was strictly prohibited at this time. He pulled a quarter of beef out of the well and the deal was made. That beef lasted us for the rest of our time in Paris.

Word came exactly as Colonel Dixon had told me. The camp was closing down six months after he told me it would. All of us were on draft for home. The Embassy put on a big party for us and then we had to get rid of any booze that we had so that turned into an all-night party. When I got back to the villa I was told that plans had been changed and rather than goining by train in the afternoon we would be flying out and the truck would be there to pick us up in ten minutes. I hadn't even started to pack and was still under the influence of the party. I crammed everything I could into my Kitbag and haversacks and managed to make it to the truck. By the time we got to the airport the weather had closed in and we sat there for a couple of hours. I t was probably a good thing because I was sobered up by then. Finally we climbed into a DC3 equipped with jump seats for paratroops and were off to London on our first leg for home.

We were billeted in a camp near London to wait for a sailing time out of Southampton. For some reason the officers of that camp treated us like new recruits. I guess they were just trying to smarten us up so we would look good when we got home. We were issued with a complete kit and put through a lot of spit and polish routine. I didn't venture far out of camp as I had only one thought on my mind and that was to get home. Marie came to say goodbye and we went to London for a weekend. It was a month before we could get a boat home. At last we boarded the Ile d'France in Southampton and were on our way. After one day at sea I think all of the brand new respirators we had been issued with went overboard. Not a word was said about it. Every one of us considered it an insult to have to carry those things after the war was over. This ship was packed with returning veterans and hundreds of war brides and their children. I enjoyed this trip with no fear of submarines or air attacks by enemy planes. It was all over now.

After 5 days at sea we emerged from a heavy fog off the coast of Newfoundland. What a wonderful sight of the sun shining on brightly painted building after seeing nothing but broken brick buildings in Europe. There wa a huge roar of delight as we sailed into Halifax Harbor. The dock was crowded with people to welcome us home. We quickly disembarked and boarded trains to take us West. This train was full of happy smiles; quite a contrast from the somber faces as we went off to war. The first major stop was Montreal and we got off the train and went across the street to a store and got some fresh fruit, something we saw little of overseas. I hadn't even seen a banana since leaving Canada.

I got off the train in Calgary and Fred met me there and we spent a week together. He was continuing his education to take up a career in Agriculture research. He was staying with a family by the name of Trollop. They were distant relative of Dads and they were very kind to us. After a week I caught the train to Edmonton and then transferred to a Greyhound bus for Viking. As it happened Eileen was on that bus. By now she was engaged to a fellow from Holden. She was teaching school there and that is where she got off the bus. We remained very good friends to the time of her death.

I got off the bus in Viking but nobody was there to meet me because they got mixed up in the time of arrival. My family had moved from the farm into town while I was away so I had to ask where they lived. No harm done as I walked in on them and what a reunion that was. My brothers had grown up and were in High School. Fay was a fine little girl and she looked at me very strangely. Who were these men coming home and having such a fuss made over them?

I had arrived home the day before the official welcome home for the local veterans. We paraded down Main Street to the Community Hall. On the way some hoodlums threw some firecrackers at us just to watch some of us, myself included, hit the dust. They were taken into hand by the local RCMP and probably got a good talking to. The banquet, prepared by the local ladies, was a feast to remember. Of course there were speeches of welcome and this was followed by a dance.

We all received a $100.00 clothing allowance when we got off the ship so now was the time to get some civilian clothes. I ordered a made-to-measure suit from the local Taylor and bought some pants and a jacket. That took most of the $100.00 I had a two week leave before I had to report to Little Mountain Barracks for discharge. There were a series of parties involving veterans as they arrived home. Ken had chopped the top off the old '28 Chev. and we tore around in that. We rarely went anywhere without having to do some repairs. Alfred and I went down to visit the old farm and had two flat tires on the way. The wiring caught fire and we were able to fix that but we sure had a good time. Alfred was still in the Army as a mechanic. He seemed to have access to a motorcycle because occasionally he came on one. We always had a good time when Alf came home.

It was soon time for me to head for Vancouver. When I arrived there I went straight to the Army Camp and went through the discharge routine. My next trip was to Vancouver Airport where I was greeted by Bill Templeton and the rest of the crew. Miss Willis was still there and she showed me a picture on the wall from the Daily Herald that showed a group of soldier resting on the roadside somewhere in Holland. I was in that picture. I was given my job back immediately and could start work in two days time. I had to find a place to live and get some work clothes. Father had been transferred to Ottawa by this time. I found a place to board on Howe Street and was all set to get back to work, My civilian clothes felt very light on me after the Army things; especially the shoes. There were a lot of changes at the Airport. The Air force was gone, the passenger planes were larger, and there were more flying clubs operating there. I very quickly fell into the routine and was just as thrilled to be there as I was before.

A beautiful young lady, Ruth, asked me one day how I would like to take flying lessons. She took me up for a familiarization flight in an Aronca Chief. I was sold and signed up with the Brisbane School of Aviation. This was it; I was doing the work I loved and flying to boot. My flying instructor was an expert and put me through all the ground instructions, i.e. air regulations, weather forecasting, care of aircraft, and many other rules a pilot must know. We went through all the flight exercises in the air and after 6 hours of flight training I felt that I could do it on my own. It was my birthday, September 11, 1946, a very calm day; I asked my instructor if I could solo. We went up for my pre- solo flight. We got to about 800 feet and he pulled the throttle. We were over the Fraser River and I set the controls for an emergency landing. There was a nice looking green area on Lulu Island and I started my decent for landing. Barry let me get right down until the tall grass tickled the landing gear. He said OK lets get out of here. I slammed on full throttle and was very glad to be out of there because I knew that would be a very rough place to land. We went up to three thousand feet and we did some stalls and spins and then landed back at the Airport. When we rolled to a stop Barry jumped out and sat down on the grass and waved me goodbye. I was on my own and followed all the rules as I moved to the take-off spot.

With a green light from the tower I pushed the throttle and was off. The first thing I noticed was how much faster I got airborne because of there was only one of us in the plane. That first circuit was wonderful and I came in for a perfect landing. From then it was practice and practice circuits and bumps.   As was the custom I had to have a solo party so I asked Ruth to be my date and I invited other pilot members and some friends to The Cave, a favorite night club down-town Vancouver. When the guys heard that I was taking Ruth they played a trick on me. They said, "Didn't you notice that Ruth always wears slacks"? They told me that one of her legs was badly disfigured. I didn't have a car at the time so I met her at the street car.   I didn't dare look at her legs until after we got to the club and she was dancing with one of the boys. Of course there was nothing wrong with her legs. We danced away the night and it was a perfect evening.

United Airlines was now flying into Vancouver and the manager was always after me to come and work for them. I talked to Bill Templeton about it and he told me that there was little chance of any advancement in my present job and that United could certainly offer promotion in the company. At last I switched over to United Airlines. They gave training lessons in all aspects of passenger service, including making out weight manifests, how to distribute baggage, getting pas-sengers through customs, operating teletype, ticket selling and many other aspects of the air transport business. We were is-sued uniforms and the pay was a bit higher.

At that time the airport café made up the in-flight meals for the airlines and this was another job for me; to see that these meals were on board. By this time I had bought a car and the manager of the café sorely wanted me to sell it to him. It was a 1937 Plymouth coupe with a rumble seat. I had paid

$550.00 for it from one of the fellows I worked with. The café manager had a 1929 Essex which seemed to be in pretty good shape. After a lot of haggling I let him have the Plymouth for the Essex and $300.00 to boot. He was moving to Winnipeg and said that he would feel much safer going through the mountains in the Plymouth.

One day George Martin called us all into the office and told us that the company was laying off 800 employees because of a strike in the States. We would be on recall in about three months. I decided to go to Edmonton as my parents had just moved there from Viking. I didn't really want to trust the Essex through the mountains either. That road was mostly gravel at that time and besides the Big Bend highway was pretty rough. I put an ad in the paper for the car stating that it had good tires. Tires were still in very short supply at the time. A fellow phoned me and said he would take the car without even asking the price. Anyhow I sold it to him for $300.50 and now I was back to using the street cars.

I packed up all my stuff and caught the train to Edmonton. I hung around for a few days but just couldn't stand being out of work. I went down town to Eaton's thinking that I could get a temporary job there. They hired me and on the first day I dressed in a suit but I was led over to the warehouse and into the appliance service shop. My first task was assembling Coffield ironers for the sales floor. The shop foreman told me that I had better get proper work clothes because I would be working on washing machines. Appliances were still in very short supply because the appliance factories had spent the war years making guns, etc. The first washing machines to arrive were Bendix automatic washers. The Bendix factory had been in full production during the war supplying the American armed forces with laundry equipment. Shipments came in by carload and I was put to work installing them. The salesmen got $23.00 for each one they sold and I was getting $25.00 a week for installing them. They had to be bolted to the floor; a very tedious job; especially on a cement floor. Two holes had to be punched in the floor and then two bolts cemented in. Three days later, after the cement had set, we had to go back and bolt the machine down and then show the owner how to use it. We didn't have a service truck, so we had to travel around on the street cars. I could do two installations in a day. There were machines to service as well. My mother still had the old Beatty washer she had on the farm. It was still in good running order but I thought she should have an automatic. When she was out I set the bolts in the floor and then had the machine delivered. I painted the old Beatty and put an ad in the paper. There was such a shortage of washing machines that a crowd of people answered the ad. I sold that machine for $100.00

It was at this time that I met a very nice girl, Elsie Lyons at a dance. We dated on and off and then one cold February night I proposed to her and a year later we were married. Our first child, Bill, was born on April 30th 1949. He was followed by 5 girls; Lynda, Judy, Donna, Caroline, and Patricia. It was a lot of work for Elsie but we are glad we have them. They are jewels.

I got very interested in my job and decided to stay with Eaton's. They had a pension plan and I was determined to improve that service department. I was of the opinion that it should be a recognized trade and provide a decent income. The first step would be to get proper tools for the job and I told the manager that, unless we got them we couldn't expect to keep up with the work. Finally he gave me an order number and told me to get what we needed. I went to Snap-on Tools

and got the very best. When the invoice came in there was
a bit of static but we could get our work done. I kept after
them until we got a service truck and then another. Now we
could divide the work into routes and really keep up with the
work. We set the shop up so that we could overhaul all of the
laundry equipment. It took seven years but I felt that I had
improved the trade and done a good service to Eaton's. Other
stores followed our way of handling the service business.

At that time Eaton's took trade-ins on new machines
and they were piling up in the warehouse. I suggested that we
overhaul them and place them on the warehouse sales floor.
This worked so well that shop staff had to be increased and
what was considered to be junk turned into low cost machines
for the public. When management realized what we were doing they offered me a promotion into the regular sales staff. I
was soon making over $100.00 a week.

We were living in a small house in Jasper Place. We had
our water trucked in and were on a septic tank that had to be
pumped several times a year. Now, with the new position we
were able to buy a new house in Holyrood on the south side of
Edmonton. We lived there for five years but I always wanted
to return to Vancouver. I asked for a transfer and we sold the
house and moved there. This was not a good move financially.
I was assigned to the furniture department but couldn't make
what I had made in Edmonton. I transferred to Trail, B.C.
but only stayed a week and saw that this wasn't an option. I
went back to Vancouver and told Elsie we were moving back
to Edmonton. I reigned from Eaton's and made plans to start
my own appliance service business

By the time we got settled in a rental house we had
$100.00 in the bank, a 1949 Dodge car, and I had a box of
tools. We had to start from home so I got a business license

and then went to see some of the business people I knew and soon had enough work to keep me busy. It was a struggle but we gradually got some good contracts and I had to hire help. I got a contract with Eaton's and had to expand the business into a shop.

During this time I joined the Appliance Serviceman's Association and became president of the organization. Our aim was to establish the trade under the apprenticeship program with the Alberta government. After years of endeavor we finally made it a reality. The government offered any of us who had ten years experience or more wouldn't have to write the exam. As president of the association I recommended that all members should take the technical courses at NAIT before writing the exam. This we did and all were successful.

Meanwhile I was becoming disenchanted with the business. There were staff problems and I seemed to be working day and night. There were no credit cards then and we had to carry a lot of receivables. Besides this it was a strain on Elsie because she looked after the books and the upkeep of the home. So it was that A1 Appliance Service was shut down and I took a job at the John Inglis Company. Two of my employees went there also. This was an eight hour day and it was like being on a holiday compared to operating a business with six employees. It was also easier having only one brand to work on.

As I worked at Inglis I got the job of trouble shooter that meant straightening out problems with customers regarding our service. One day I had to go to the school board to sort out a problem with billing. While I was there a gentleman beckoned me into his office. He asked me, "How would you like to come and teach for us? We are building a new vocational school and would like to offer an appliance service course". I thanked him and told him that I had not completed high school; let alone university. He told me that they had a program whereby I could finish my matriculation and get one year of university. The government would pay me while I went to school and besides I would get a temporary teaching certificate after the year of university and only needed two more years to get my degree. In other words I could start teaching with the temporary certificate and complete my degree at night school and summer school. This program would be starting a year hence. I explained that I had six kids at home and it would be a pretty heavy load. Anyhow I told him to put my name down on the list and I would think about it.

A year later I was at a customer's home and got an urgent message to call home. I hadn't told Elsie about the teaching job because it seemed to me to be out of the question. When I phoned her she said, "What's all this about you starting school on Wednesday"? I told her that I had better come home right now. When I told her about it she said, "If you want to do this I will go to work and we will manage somehow. I phoned the college and said that I would have to give notice at work. The reply was, "Either be here on Wednesday or your name will go to the bottom of the list". I phoned my boss and he thanked me for all the notice but wished me well. On my last day at work Don gave me a key to the shop and said, "You know what has to be done so come in any time you want and leave your time on my desk, even if it is two o'clock in the morning. This was the beginning of a new venture.

At the college I found myself in classes with young people completing their studies and other tradesmen doing the same. Actually I fell into my studies as though I had never left school. Elsie got a part time job and we got along fine. I got very good marks and the time seemed to fly. I passed my matriculation, skipping many of the preliminary courses and going straight to grade 12 level courses. In September I was off to the University of Alberta. My tuition was paid by the government and we were able to scrape by on my living allowance. Elsie's income topped it off and we moved ahead.

I got my temporary teaching certificate and went to the school board and I was told that they were not hiring that year. Thankfully Don Cameron rehired me and I carried on at Inglis for another year. I got a call 3 days before school opening to come in for an interview. A teaching position was open for me at Victoria Composite High School. This time I had to give short notice to a new manager at Inglis but he wished me well and said there would be work for me there any time I needed it.

The Appliance Service course did not materialize so I took on a course in general metals that included welding and metal work. I knew how to do basic welding but was not a qualified welder. The senior welding teacher was teaching a night course and I enrolled so that now I was teaching all day, going to university three nights a week, and to my welding class the other two nights. It was a strain but I weathered the storm. I loved teaching and feel that I influenced the lives of many young people. Many of them went on to be qualified tradesmen.

It took seven years to graduate from university with a degree in vocational education but was well worth the effort. The day I wrote my last exam I went home and threw a book in the corner and said, "Let's go on a holiday"!! Our youngest daughter, Patricia said, "Let's go to Disneyland"! The next day I hooked up the tent trailer and we were off. Trish invited a girl friend to come along for company. The other children had left home by now so the four of us had a wonderful holiday.

I was now in a higher pay group and we could do many things we wanted to do. Elsie and I bought a new holiday trailer and the next summer set off on a trip to Newfoundland. Fred had taken a job there as an agriculture research scientist. We had two months and took our time as we explored many historical places on the way. Some people said that it would be a boring trip across Canada but we found something to see everywhere we went. Every Canadian should have this experience. This trip and two other trips across Canada sewed the seed for my book, *Camp Vernon A Century of Canadian Military History*.

For the first seven years of my teaching career I had only male students but then girls were introduced. This put a whole new flavor on teaching. In my welding classes I found that the girls seemed to have a very artistic approach to that art and they turned out some very good work. They were not so good when it came to cutting out sheet metal projects. I had to pay quite a bit more attention to discipline with the girls. Of course they were at the age of change and didn't always have their minds on their studies. I ran a pretty tight ship in my courses and found that my students preferred my classes to those where the teacher gave them a free hand. I had an expression that, "kids are starving for discipline'" and to this day I believe it. My classes were always full. I didn't kick kids out of my classes and handled most of the counseling myself. I am satisfied that it worked.

At the outset our students were identified as slow learners and we soon found out that our program became the dumping ground for kids with bad behavior. We Vocies, as we were called, were older teachers and were able to deal with all types of students. Victoria Composite had students of all races and at one time I was called upon to substitute for the teacher who taught English as a second language. Now this was a challenge but I enjoyed it. There were five different nationalities in the class. It was just for a few weeks so I was able to get through it and quite enjoyed it. After ten years of teaching I was called upon to join the math team. I and another teacher actually wrote a math course suitable for vocational courses. Some of these kids were in grade ten and didn't know the first thing about fractions so we started from the very beginning; how our numbering system works right up to simple algebra. This made courses like machine shop and carpentry much easier to teach.

At the end of my thirteenth year the government decided that vocational education was too costly and started closing down the shops. In my mind this was foolish because in later years there was a great shortage of tradesmen and industry had to hire offshore tradesmen to fill the demand.

During the next two years I found the job to be very frustrating because I was pushed into teaching courses that were beyond my expertise. It got bad enough that I was forced to take a couple of month's sick leave. I carried on but knew that it was getting to me. We had overloaded classes and no support from administration. Strikes were threatened but nothing was done about it. I was now 53 years of age and started thinking about early retirement. When I came back from my second sick leave I was given the job of substitute teaching. I got full pay but had to travel all over the city and more often than not there was no lesson plan left by the teacher I was replacing. Finally I threw in the towel and took long time sick leave. I refused to retire so they had to give me full pay until age sixty five. I have no regrets about teaching. I loved it and wished that I could have carried on for a few more years.

That first winter Elsie and I traveled to Arizona for a holiday with a couple of friends. We stayed in a very nice hotel in Phoenix, rented a car and had a wonderful sight seeing experience. We went to se Montezuma castle where a tribe of natives lived in caves built into the cliffs. Access was by ladders and evidence shows that they lived a good life. We went to Los Angeles and to Disneyland, Sea land, Universal Studios, and many other famous places. We drove to Santiago and visited the Wildlife Zoo and crossed the border to Mexico by bus. Tijuana gave us a glimpse of real poverty. We had fun haggling over things to buy and then headed back to Los Angeles. We stopped by to see the Spruce Goose, the famous plane built for Howard Hughes. We then headed eastward to Phoenix. One night we went to a square dance and there were six other couples from our club there. We had a great time and after the dance we all went out to eat in a restaurant in Scottsdale. It was run by a group of university students and, by reputation, they were more than generous with their servings. I ordered a hamburger and when it came it covered a large plate and had a ring of fried potato slices around the outside. I really had to force it down and then one member of the group suggested a desert. Not to be left out, I ordered a sundae. Now this was the biggest sundae I have ever seen. We returned to our hotel and prepared for the return trip home. Donna met us at the Airport in Edmonton in the midst of a blizzard. It was a wonderful holiday.

We had purchased a cabin at Sandy Lake from Mother's estate and spent most weekends there while I was teaching. It was so nice and quiet there and we spent many hours cruising around on the lake in our boat. We loved going around an island through the reeds and could see the nests of the water fowl a few feet away. We were watching television one night and it suddenly went off. The next morning I set about finding what went wrong. I climbed into the attic and amongst the shavings I found the trouble. The wiring was the knob and tube variety and at one splice the insulation had burned back about an inch. That we didn't burn down was a miracle. That day I set about to rewire the whole cabin. At the same time I had a 220 volt line put in so that we could have an electric stove. I also found that there was no insulation in the walls.

With the help of Judy's husband, Bob Hidson we went to work remodeling the cabin. We had remodeled our house in town and had replaced the windows and doors so we hauled the old ones out to the lake and went to work removing the siding. We could now put proper insulation in and install the windows and doors in their new locations. I was building a new tool shed and used two of the windows on that building. I also installed one of the overhead doors from the garage on the tool shed. The drywall in the bedroom was in bad shape so we took that down and put in new drywall.

Now that I wasn't working we could spent much of our time at the lake. The next door neighbor had a bob cat and he dug us a proper septic tank for the outdoor toilet. We cut down some trees and seeded grass so the place was getting to look pretty nice. It was a nice community and they had some social functions there. There was a store at the entrance to the lake . We could get our groceries there saving hauling them from town. It was a great place for our children. They were able to have a swim each morning before breakfast; prodded on by me.

We had frequent visitors at the lake. Some came just before supper and left before the dishes were done but most did help out and we enjoyed the company. I still look back on those days at the lake with great pleasure and wonder what it would have been like to make it a permanent residence. Elsie and I talked about it and even got estimates from a local contractor. Lynda and Don had moved to the Okanogan and wanted us to move there. We often talked about it and seriously considered moving there. In the winter we went out to the lake and stoked up the fire and spent some time there. We even did some ice fishing with not much luck but it was another experience. As spring came the road got almost impassable and that threw some doubts on building there. One evening I said to Elsie, "Let's sleep on it and whatever decision we come to, that is what we will do". Thus came the decision to move to Vernon.

We listed our house for sale and it sold very quickly and before we wanted to make the move. We packed everything up and placed in storage and moved in with Donna. This worked out very well and by the middle of May we were ready to move on. We went to Vernon to find a place to rent. We found a town house called Green Timbers and rented it. We didn't want to buy a house until we knew we would like Vernon. At the beginning of May we loaded our stuff into a U-haul truck and Warren drove it to Vernon. Elsie drove our K-car and I drove the truck with a trailer load of stuff. It was a nice warm day when we arrived in Vernon and moved into the town house. It was a comfortable place, two bedrooms, and a full basement. There was also an outdoor swimming pool which was very nice because it was a very hot summer.

We stayed in the apartment for six months and then started looking for a house. We found a nice three bedroom house on 24th Avenue on the East Hill, a very respectable district in Vernon. We bought it and got right to work on renovating it. There was an ugly acorn fireplace in the living room and half an hour after we got there it was gone. We replaced carpets, the furnace and hot water heater, and many other changes to suit us. We had the ceilings re-stippled and the whole interior of the house repainted. There was a big garage and workshop, some fruit trees, and a large garden. In the garage was a cold room where we could keep preserves and vegetables even in the winter time. It was very well insulated and I hooked up a 300 watt light bulb with a thermostat to keep it from freezing. We had cherries, apples, peaches, and plums so we had plenty of deserts and jams to store in the cold room. We were very comfortable there and enjoyed the neighborhood. One of the first things we noticed about Vernon was that it was small enough that it didn't take more than ten minutes to get anywhere. After Edmonton we were always arriving at our appointments about half an hour early.

Chapter Eight

Don and Lynda had moved to Vernon from Hinton Alberta where Don had a Snap-on Tool agency. After a short time here he sold the agency and bought into a partnership called Okanagan Tractor where they overhauled heavy duty logging equipment and sold parts. I took over the parts department the odd time when Don had to be away. A couple of years later Don got out of that business and was looking for something else.

On a visit to Edmonton I went to visit a friend of mine at the Electricians Union and as I sat in his office the girls in the office suddenly grabbed their purses and said, "Here comes the Nutman"! A chap came in with a basket of bagged nuts, candies, and other goodies. In a matter of a few minutes the guy had sold $30.00 worth of stuff and was on his way to the next business. I got the Nutman address and when I returned to Vernon I told Don about it. The next thing we were on the way to Edmonton to explore the possibility of opening a franchise in the Okanagan. Don got the franchise and set up shop in his home.

This business was an instant success. I helped him open accounts in Vernon, Kamloops, Kelowna, Penticton, and Salmon Arm. He hired a couple of salesmen and a girl to help

bag and label product. Lynda made up beautiful gift baskets
for the holiday seasons. It got so busy that Elsie and I joined
in to help out when the load got too heavy. It was a lot of fun
and a booming business. Don was a good business man and
did well for a number of years.

Elsie and I joined the Anglican Church congregation an
attended services regularly. We met many new friends there
and I joined the Men's group and worked on projects around
the Church. Elsie joined a Guild so we were kept pretty busy.
We transferred our Legion membership to Branch 25 here
in Vernon and it wasn't long before I was on the executive
committee. I went on the visiting committee dropping in on
veterans in care centers. The numbers grew to over 100 vets. I
had to see every week. I needed help and finally got two other
Legionnaires to help out. Elsie was elected to President of St.
Theresa's guild and she was kept busy on their projects. In fact
that led me to my first crack at writing. They wanted a parish
book with stories from each of the parishioners. I wrote up
the stories on my computer and then they were put together
into a book. The Church sorely needed a new parish hall and
I got quite involved with that.

In 1990 I suggested to Elsie that we take an open ended
holiday and travel for a year. We had never traveled down the
east coast of North America. The first concern was how could
we do it? I explained to Elsie that we could sell the house and
again put out stuff into storage and then buy another house
upon our return. This seemed like a preposterous idea to Elsie
as she said, "What will we do with the dogs"? I replied, "We
will take it with us"! We talked about it until it seemed to
make sense and finally decided to do it.

We listed the house for sale in April and it sold right
away so we had to do some fast preparations to leave at the

beginning of May. We bought a brand new 25 foot 5th wheel and a used super cab truck. We got the truck painted to match the trailer and had an air conditioner installed in the trailer. Then we had the truck thoroughly checked over at the Ford garage. We had a garage sale and got rid of a lot of stuff and put the rest in storage. Now all we had to do was settle our affairs, i.e. mail, credit accounts, etc, load up the trailer and we were ready to start out, dogs and all.

I had built a large box for the dogs and placed it on the back seat so they were comfortable. Chrissie and her pup, Tripper, were long hair dachshunds and were used to traveling so were very little trouble to us. On a lovely sunny day, May 1st. we waved goodbye to the house and started our long journey. Our first stop was Edmonton and we parked the unit at Judy's house. The brakes on the truck seemed to be acting up so I took it to a brake shop and they were completely shot. Even the drums had to be replaced. So much for the big check over in Vernon. The second night we were there Judy got a phone call that Trish and Allen had been in a terrible car crash and they and the two children were in hospital. We rushed over there to find that Trish was in critical condition with a broken neck. Allen and the kids were released from hospital the next day and we went to their house to look after things. We stayed there for a month until we were certain that Trish was on the mend. Allen's mom came in to take over from us and we were on the way again.

As we were pulling into Lloydminister, the truck was sputtering and losing power. It was a holiday weekend so there were no mechanics on duty. We visited with Len Lafoy, an Army buddy of mine, and we had a great time. I figured it was a dirty fuel pump but the mechanic thought it was ignition trouble. I insisted on a new fuel filter and got under way.

A few miles down the road it started acting up again and I got the mechanic to take the carburetor apart and he found a small piece of cork from the gasket in the jet. With that fixed we had no more trouble and went on to Saskatoon. As planned we went to the tourist office of each major city we came to and if there were a bus tour or a boat tour we took it. We took the bus tour in Saskatoon and stayed there for a couple of days to see all the sights. There was no hurry and no appointments. We could just take our time.

We turned south to Regina and did the same thing. We even stopped in to Outlook Saskatchewan to visit a retired teacher friend of mine. He was a well known artist and we stayed over there for a day before moving on to Manitoba. Some people say there is nothing to see in the Prairie Provinces. This is totally untrue and we thoroughly enjoyed this part of our trip. Traveling is a great educator as we discovered. Every Canadian should travel across this great country and see what a wealth nation we have. Historical sights are everywhere..

We toured Winnipeg, taking a boat tour on the Red River and a city bus tour. We went out to St. Boniface and saw a refurbished fur trading post and many artifacts from the early days in that Province.

It might be added that Winnipeg is very rich in mosquitoes as well. We moved on to the huge Province of Ontario, the land of forests, lakes. rock and rich farm land. It took us six days to cross as far as Ottawa, our capitol. We spent a week here seeing all the sights, including the Parliament Buildings. We took a boat tour on the Redeau Canal and a bus tour of the city. From there it was to Quebec City and another bus tour. This quaint old French city has so much Canadian history to show off to thousands of tourists. On this trip we went right around the Cape and stopped at Perce Rock, a famous Canadian site jutting out into the Atlantic Ocean. We took a boat ride over to Bonaventure Island and saw the gannets by the thousands. The are a large white seabird and crowd themselves together with about a square foot each where they lay their eggs and raise the young. It is a wonder that they can find their spot when they return from a fishing trip to feed the young.

Our next point of interest was New Brunswick's beautiful coastline and then of course we had to visit Monkton and the magnetic hill as well as the tidal bore on the St. Johns River. By the end of July we were in Nova Scotia and traveled to Halifax and then followed the coast to Peggy's Cove and other neat little bays and fishing villages. We visited Digby, famous for their scallops and other seafood. Next we drove around the Cabot Trail, a days trip of rugged coast and ever-changing scenery. The smell of the wild roses and the ever-present sea water. It was here we tasted the finest of clam chowder.

We went over to Prince Edward Island and toured the whole island. Once again we had to see the live production of Anne of Green Gables in Charlottown. I took an early morning deep sea fishing trip and brought back to the trailer some fresh cod fish. While we were there Tripper got hold of my glasses and chewed them so we had to go into Charlottown for a new pair. It was just another one of those things that happen on a trip. We just had to go back and see Green Gables and have a swim at Rustico Beach. I don't know what that Island is like in the winter time but it is beautiful in the summer.

We caught the ferry back to New Brunswick and then drove on to North Sydney. Here we went to visit the site where Marconi sent his first radio message overseas. We spent the night parked on the ferry dock to catch the ferry for Port

Eau Basque the next day. The sea was a little rough and Elsie got a little sea sick but survived the trip. Now was the time for the long trip across Newfoundland to St. John. I think this was the best bit of highway we had seen so far. The Canadian Government gave them this as a replacement for the railway line with its narrow gauge rails and the famous bullet. We took our time on this trip so that we could take in the wonderful scenery and the ever changing landscape. At one point we would be passing through a wooded area and the next passing a little bay with fishing boats and piles of lobster traps. Always present was the smell of the sea and mile after mile of rocky terrain. We parked our rig in a camp ground and stayed wit h Fred and Peggy for about ten days. This was another wonderful time. We went on a fishing boat out to Bird Island to see the puffins and other sea birds. There were huge icebergs out there.. W went to a couple of seafood places and savored the different kinds of fish and mollusks. To return to the mainland we took the long way and were at sea overnight. Again Elsie felt a bit seasick and spent quite a bit of time in her bunk. I have never been seasick myself but it must be awful.

We arrived back in North Sidney and took time to straighten out things in the trailer. By this time we knew that we brought along too much gear. However, being late September the weather was getting a bit chilly and we were glad we brought along our winter coats. Also at this time the fall colors were starting to come out. I don't think there is anywhere else in Canada that displays such beauty at this time of year. We drove down to St. Johns new Brunswick to view the reversing falls on the St. Johns River. When the tide comes in the water backs up the river and boats can go up stream and when the tide goes out the water is too low for boats and the river water is seen flowing to the sea.

We had to leave there because they were closing down the camp ground for the season so we headed up to Fredericton. This is an interesting city and the seat of the Provincial Government. We went to see their parliament buildings as we did in each capitol city as we traveled across Canada. We set up camp at Kings Landing, the site where Loyalists settled and lived in a close knit farming community along the St.John River. They were celebrating Canadian Thanksgiving Day and served up a wonderful turkey dinner with all the trimmings. It was getting colder and we were becoming anxious to move south. We crossed the border into Maine on the 10th of October. We passed through a wooded area with all the fall beauty at its best. There were lakes and rivers and then we got into blue hill country and on to New York State. We parked about 30 miles from New York City and took a bus tour from the KOA campsite. The staff looked after our dogs while we were away. This was a wonderful and well organized tour. We went to Arlington Cemetery and saw the graves of JFK, his brother, and Joe Lewis as well as many other dignitaries. We went up in the Statue of Liberty. What a wonderful guardian of New York Harbor. At noon we went up in the Empire State Building and from the 87th floor we could view all the famous sights for miles around. We even got to go into the White House and see the Oval Office. We saw the Canadian War Memorial erected in honor of Canadians who served in the American Army.

The next day we were parked about 20 miles from Washington DC. This was as close as one could find a camp site. It was a KOA and again they looked after our dogs while we were on tour. We saw the Crying Wall and many other points of interest, including a tour of the black ghetto area. Three quarters of the population of Washington is black. We drove out to see the Roosevelt estate and the graves of him and his wife. His home is now a National Monument visited by thousands of tourists from around the world. In the yard is the most beautiful maple tree I have ever seen. Of course it was in its fall colors too.

While we were there it was Halloween and the trick or treaters were out. We had picked up some treats and handed them out at the door of our trailer. I took the dogs for a walk and what should come by but a mother skunk and her brood of young ones. Fortunately the dogs did not see them. I could just imagine what it would have been like it they got skunked up and had to ride with us. In the States Halloween is celebrated for a whole month and the people go all out to decorate their yards with spooks and othe paraphernalia for the season.

We rolled on down to Williamsburg, a significant site in American history. This is where the War of Independence ended. Parts of he city have been refurbished to its original state and tourists can ride on miniature trains to view the old shops. Many of the old trades, such as the blacksmith's shop and an old school are displayed. The Old fort is there as well but we didn't take the time to go through it. We were getting pretty tired and needed a break so we took a day off to stay in camp. We were getting further south and, although the weather was getting warmer, the fall colors were following us.

The next stop was Myrtle Beach and this is where we saw our first palm trees. We decided to stop there for awhile. There was seven miles of sandy beach and the water to us was warm. For the locals it was winter and we had the beach pretty well to ourselves. In Washington we had met a Doctor and his wife from B.C. Surprise, surprise they were camped next to us at Myrtle Beach. We visited back and forth and played cards with them. It was nice to have company from home. While we were there we got the tuck serviced and went to an RV shop and bought a carpet to lay out in front of the trailer and some other trailer stuff. I don't think we ever walked out of one of those places without buying something.

We were now getting down into the country where the big estates were located. Some were open for tourists and it was interesting to see how they lived. The owners had black slaves and grew cotton and sugar cane. The kitchen was separate from the house as a precaution against fire. The further south we got the more we noticed the American drawl in their speech. We passed through the Virginias and Carolinas to Florida. We started seeing huge groves of orange trees loaded with oranges. The weather was very warm and we could store away all winter clothes. We spent a month in Florida and took in many sights and events. We went to Disney World, the Epcot Center, Sea world, and out to Cape Canaveral. We even saw a space craft lift-off One day we drove to Viscaya a millionaire estate of the farm machinery company owner, Dearing of McCormick Dearing fame. Father had some Dearing machines on the farm at Rodino. The ceilings of this place were plated with gold and he had a private dock where his friends could dock their Yachts when they came for a visit. There were about ten guest rooms and luxury was everywhere. The grounds were manicured with shaped hedges and beds of beautiful flowers. The motif, we were told was 16th Century Italian Renaissance. This estate is now a National Monument

We drove along a road parallel to the beaches of Miami but could only get a glimpse of them because they were mostly hidden by rows and rows of beach apartments. We stopped at Fort Lauderdale and met Elsie's sister there who was about to board a cruise ship to travel to the Panama Canal. We were going to travel down the Keyes but were told that it would be difficult to find a camp spot big enough for our rig. Ridiculous!!! Any how we headed west across the Everglades; really a very slow moving river moving to the Gulf of Mexico. The highway was built on miles and miles of floating bridges. We were not feeling up to snuff that day so passed up the swamp boat tours. We saw many different members of wildlife including Aligators, white ibis, grey herons, vultures, and many others. We arrived at Fort Myers that night a got settled in a very nice KOA campground. As we walked the dogs here we noticed signs telling people to keep their dogs well away from the ponds because alligators could leap out and grab them; not a bad warning for us either. Fort Myers was the summer home for Henry Ford, B.F. Goodrich, and Thomas Edison. Their homes were side by side and it seems they worked together there on many of their inventions. Edison's huge laboratory is still there and now displays many of his inventions. During the war he worked with B.F. Goodrich of a substitute for rubber to make tires. They needed to find some plant that produced enough latex and after much experimenting came up with golden rod which grows very tall and abundantly in Florida.

Henry Ford had a long dock in front of his place and was often seen sitting at the end of it apparently fishing but the truth of it was that he went there to do his thinking at a place he would not be disturbed. In the lab sat one of his earliest model T cars he had given to Edison as a gift and as he improved he added those improvements to that car. This was a very nice place and we stayed there for a week. As we moved on through the country we notice large masses of moss in the trees, Henry Ford used this to stuff the cushions in his cars. It is now used to support the flowers in potted arrangements. As we moved on we saw a sign that indicated the Steven Foster Culture Center at Live Oaks. It was about 50 miles off our route but we decided to go there. It was late in the day so we decided to camp for the night a few miles from Live Oaks. To our surprise we discovered that we were camped on the bank of the Sewanee River so famous in one of Foster's songs. The next morning we drove to Live Oaks and were lucky to be there for a country fair. Many of the local crafts were on display there such as; making peanut brittle, a mobile sawmill, and there was a display of making sugar from sugar cane. In the main building Steven Foster's songs were depicted in 8 dioramas. For The Old Folks at Home there was a cozy looking cottage with smoke rising from the chimney. Steven Foster grew up in Illinois and never saw the Sewanee River. He had enlisted the help of his niece to find the name of an American river that fit into his song and that is the one she came up with. We stayed there for the whole day and then headed west again.

A colleague of mine at Victoria Composite High School had mentioned to me at my retirement party that she was going to take a post- graduate course at the University of Tallahassee. We were going right through there so looked her up and went out for a very nice dinner with her and her husband. It was nice to see her so far from home.

As we drove along the Gulf of Mexico we saw miles of white sand. We stopped at Panama City for a swim in the Gulf. The water was nice and warm. In the camp site crushed sea shells were used in place of gravel; a little hard on the feet I walked on with no shoes. Our next stop was just outside of Houston where we stayed for three days. We visited the NASA Space Center and actually got to go into Mission Control. There was little activity there that day so we were allowed to sit where the astronaut's family would sit during a return from space. We toured that huge city and saw the 80,000 seat Super Drome and learned that the air conditioning in that building must be left on all the time; otherwise clouds would form inside and it would rain in there.

We crossed the border into Mississippi ad camped near New Orleans. We drove the truck across the Ponchartrain and then took a bus tour of the city. That bridge is 24 miles long and from the center, neither shore can be seen. We saw a graveyard where the caskets are above the surface because if they were buried they would only rise to the surface because of the high water table. We strolled around the French quarter where the French are called Cajuns. We boarded a paddle wheeler for a tour of the second larges port in the United States.

It was getting into November and we had made a tentative date to meet the Fitzpatrick's in San Antonio on November 19th. When we were traveling through Houston the news was all about Thanksgiving and Christmas. In fact we saw a Santa Clause descending in a parachute at some community. Huston is a huge oil city and there are miles of oil pumpers along the coast of the Gulf of Mexico. The freeway through Huston is a marvel. I set the cruise control at 90mph and didn't have to stop for a single red light for 100 miles. We arrived at San Antonio on thanksgiving eave and went into town for a big thanksgiving dinner. We phoned our friends in Phoenix where they were holidaying but they said they couldn't meet us there. It was a bit of a disappointment but we would see them when we got to Phoenix. In our Camp ground we noticed that the leaves were falling off the trees and already the new ones were budding out. There is a winding river through the town and colorful boats are used as part of their transit system. There are souvenir shops and cafes all along the way. We took a round trip on one of the boats and then stopped for lunch at a little lunch place. Just as we left there Elsie noticed that she didn't have her purse and thought that she must have left it on the boat. When we got back to camp there it was on the table. That night there was to be a Santa Clause Parade of boats on the river. We were advised to get ther by five o'clock if we expected to get a view spot by the railing. People came from far and wide for this spectacular sight. We took the local bus so we didn't have to worry about parking and were in plenty of time for a front line view. When it got dark the boats came all lined up and decorated with thousands of lights. Each boat had a generator to supply the electricity for the lights. In the front boat was good old St. Nicolas waving to the cheering crowd. When we were standing there we got into conversation with a local couple and the volunteered to drive us back to camp after the show. Good old southern hospitality!!

The next day we went to see the Alamo where a few Americans led by Davie Crocket held out against the Mexicans'. All of them were slaughtered but it stopped the Mexicans until reinforcements came to turn the tide of battle in the Mexican War. We had to remove our shoes in respect for those brave men who so heroically held out against such odds.

As we drove on we saw a sign directing us to the Carlsbad Caves in New Mexico. We had nothing but time and headed up there. These caves are famous for their enormous size and the millions of bats that make their home there. We spent a couple of days there exploring that strange place and then set out for El Paso and Arizona. There was a very strong headwind and a steady rise in the land right to the Texas, Arizona border. At times I thought that there was trouble with the truck but once we got to El Paso the wind died down and the road leveled out so we were OK. We camped at El Paso and then proceeded to Apache Junction just outside of Mesa. The Fitzpatrick's met us here and on the following day we found a very nice holiday trailer park called Tower Point. It was said to be the nicest one in Mesa which is part of Phoenix.

We got the trailer hooked up to power, water, sewer, cable, and even had a telephone connected. This was December and it got quite cold at nights. It even snowed in the desert and our water lines froze a couple of times. We had a pleasant surprise when Donna came down to stay for Christmas. One day we took the dogs for a walk along the canal and let them off leash to have a run. Tripper was chasing Chrissie and slipped into the canal. I scrambled down the steep bank to help him out and he just continued with his chase as though nothing had happened. We decorated our unit for Christmas and the complex supplied everybody with paper bags and candles. We lit the candles and placed them in the bags and lined them up across the front of our lot and when they were all set out it made very show of lights for the whole complex. A big Christmas party was held at the main hall. Elsie and Donna and I were invited to the Fitzpatrick's for Christmas dinner. Another couple; friends of ours from Vernon, Ken and Nora Gee were in another park were also invited and we were treated to turkey with all the trimmings. We stuffed ourselves as usual and enjoyed a very nice Christmas. We did some sight seeing with Donna and did some shopping at some of the malls. When Donna left for home we started thinking about moving on. We were to meet Judy and Jack at Palm Springs for New Year's Day. We got packed up and checked out on December 27th and headed west.

We checked into a very nice camp ground in Palm Springs and Judy and Jack were there with Jack's daughter Sam and Judy's son Tom. We took daily dips in the hot tub and toured around this beautiful resort. Bob Hope's mansion was in full view from our site. We took the gondola up the mountain and the view was spectacular. We went over to visit a date farm and spent most of a day there. We bought a good supply of the best dates we had ever tasted.

Jack's sister had made arrangements for all of us to meet their cousin for a New Year's dinner. John and Monica put on a spread such as I have vever seen before or since. We had a very enjoyable visit with them and then returned to our camp site. The truck gave us some more trouble here. It wouldn't pull at all but we managed to coax it to a small country garage run by two brothers. They determined that the torque converter was shot. One of them said, "I think we have one of those out on a wreck outside. Sure enough it was one that fit our truck and they gave it to us installed for $40.00, a steal if they had charged twice that much.

The next adventure was a trip to the San Diego Wild animal Park. Here we boarded a special sight-seeing train and we rode around the park in perfect comfort. The animals were loose in large pastures free to roam as they pleased. It was so nice to see them this way rather than cooped up in cages as they are in most zoos. That evening we all went out for supper and said our goodbyes as we were heading north the next morning. Elsie was getting anxious to be home as it was over 8 months since we left. We spent a day in Los Angeles and then to the coast road north on 1-101 to San Francisco. It was a wet dreary day as we crossed the Golden Gate Bridge.

We could hardly make out Alcatraz, the famous maximum security prison.

We continued on to Petula and the Redwood Forest. We saw a tree that stood 367.9 feet tall and was estimated to be 580 years old. This is a spectacular sight indeed. We noticed that the weather was getting colder and the furnace in the trailer ran almost continuously. In Coos Bay, Oregon we stopped at a specialty shop where they sold myrtle wood items. It is a very hard wood with a very fine and pretty grain, suitable for making ornaments. It will only grow in Oregon in the Western Hemisphere. We bought a few items for gifts and a few for ourselves. We noticed a sign advertising RV anti-freeze at a very low price so we got enough to winterize the unit before we froze some water pipes. We also made sure the truck radiator was properly prepared for cold weather.

When we got to Seattle it was pouring rain and the camp ground was like a swamp. This was the last night we slept in the trailer as the rain turned to sleet. By the time we got to Bellingham a foot of snow had fallen and the highway was in terrible condition. We went over a very icy stretch of highway to the border where we had to go through customs. This wasn't too bad except that we had to wade through knee deep snow to get into the place. We had all our purchases listed in American dollars and they said that it had to be in Canadian dollars. I wasn't in the mood to do the math so I just estimated it and handed it in. It passed and we were on our way. The road from here to Merritt was plowed out so that part was easy except at Hope. We stopped there for lunch and I got stuck in the parking lot. Some guys were passing by in a sand truck and they threw me a couple of shovels full and we were free. We pulled into Merritt for the night and just parked the unit and went into a motel. In the morning the temperature was -20 C so it is a good thing we had winterized the trailer. As we headed over the connector we ran into fog. The road was icy in spots but not too bad but I was fearful of the fog. We got through to Kelowna and it was clear sailing from there to Vernon. We got the trailer parked and then drove up to Lynda and Don's place where we would stay until we got another house. This ended a very long and enjoyable trip of 21,470 miles. We took many pictures on the trip to remind us of the wonderful time we had.

Our car was buried in snow and when I got it dug out it started at first try. The mice had got into it and stored about five pounds of corn in the trunk. Don still had his Nutman business going and we carried on giving him a hand with that. It took some getting used to living in a house again and were anxious to find a place of our own.

Chapter Nine

We contacted our real estate agent, Don Defeo and he showed as number of properties but nothing that was suitable. A former neighbor of Lynda's was selling his house in the East Hill district and we made an appointment to see it. The owner told us that he had intended to do some renovations on it before selling. I offered to buy it as is and at a reduced price and then we would be able to fix it up the way we wanted it. He agreed and lowered the price accordingly. It was a three bedroom split level with a half basement, half crawl space, and a good size lot. There were 3 huge Lombardy poplars and some unruly shrubs in the back yard. There was also a golden delicious apple tree there and two large birch trees that were dying in the front yard. The back deck was rotten and needed replacing so there was a lot to do.

This was a very well built house and though it needed a lot of work, we were able to move in right away. We had our stuff moved from storage and unloaded the 5th wheel into the house. It was then that we realized how much unnecessary stuff we had taken with us. I found a bottle of wine tucked away that we had bought in Vernon.

As soon as we got settled in we started on the renovation. I took charge of finding tradesmen to do the work and did a great deal of it myself. The first thing was to add insulation to the attic and replace the patio door off the dining room. We hired a carpenter to rebuild the deck and put a roof on it so now we could enjoy sitting outside. We got hold of a tree cutter and got all the trees removed except the apple tree. I upgraded the wiring and made plans for a garage and a new driveway.

The next spring we got the driveway and sidewalks and the foundation for the garage poured. At the same time we had the lawn dug out and new sod laid. Bill came from Calgary and helped me build the garage. Now it was time to start on the inside of the house. Elsie picked out new drapes and curtains. She also chose the colors for a complete paint job in all the upstairs and main floor rooms. It took a bit of looking around to get the right carpeting for the living room and bedrooms.

We had a good year for apples and got at least60 pounds of them. There was a small garden but it was overgrown with weeds and it took most of the summer to get that in shape. The garden shed floor was not in good shape but that and the outside painting would have to wait till next spring. In the meantime I wired the garage and repaired the fence in the back yard. When all of this was done we had a very comfortable home with the renovation costing just over $30,000.00. We considered it a worthwhile investment and would later recoup this money.

We got word that Alfred was having angina pain and had to have by-pass surgery. About the same time I got a terrible pain in my back and was told I had a kidney stone and was sent to Vancouver for ultrasound treatment. With that fixed I was able to carry on as usual.

Elsie's mom was in an extended care facility and not able to go out on her own so we brought her to Vernon for a short spell. On her return to Edmonton she continued to fail and in October we went to visit her for the last time. We were with her when she passed away. Margaret was in hospital at the time and couldn't attend her mother's funeral. It was not long after this that I started having angina pain and was put on a waiting list for angioplasty surgery. Three months later I was off to Vancouver for the procedure and felt much better.

In the spring of 1991 Judy and Jack came out for a visit. Judy wanted to move here after her retirement 10 years hence. They looked around and found acreage At Sunset Properties, a district about 13 miles from town. It overlooked Lake Okanagan and was situated on the side of a mountain. It was heavily wooded and had no buildings on it.

One day I was talking to Judy on the phone and asked her what she was going to do with that property and she said that they might put up a double garage and when they came out on holidays they could store their boat and other stuff in it. Off-handedly I said, "Why don't I build a house on it and we could live there and develop the property so that it would be all fixed up by the time you and Jack retire". A few days later Judy called me and asked me if I were serious about my suggestion. I told her that we should be able to work out some kind of a deal and the next week she came out with a set of plans. She hired Roy Reeves, a building contractor and asked me to oversee the job. Elsie and I decided to sell our house and thus have the funds to build the house. The deal was that Judy wouldn't charge us any rent for living there and we would not charge her any interest. I would work at developing the property and adding any improvements at her expense. We wrote up a five year contract and we were ready to go to work.

It took until September to get all the permits in order and Roy got going with digging out the basement. He was a very easy man to work with and he added many suggestions to make it a very sturdy building. Because of delays in getting permits we were into late fall and the snow came before the house was closed in. However with a few other snags the house was ready for us to move into in early March. We got a good price for our house and were able to pay outright for the new building. In the summer Judy and Jack came out and we worked together on several projects, i.e. installing lights at the entrances of the driveway, building steps down the sides of the house, and planting the tiered bank from the road down to the house. I had hired a contractor to shape the bank and pave the driveway, Elsie and Judy had selected drapes and curtains for the windows. I got to work designing a cold room, a laundry room, a bathroom and two bedrooms in the basement. Now we had three bathrooms for the two of us and to think that we raised six kids with only one. We built framed up the rooms and got contractors in to drywall and lay carpet and linoleum in these rooms. Now there were two bedrooms in the basement, two bedrooms on the main floor, and a bedroom in the loft overlooking the main living room. Large windows faced the lake and a deck surrounded two sides of the house on both levels. It had a walk- out entrance to the covered lower deck. The deck on the north side of the house was also covered with a patio door from the space between the kitchen and dining room. Included in the complex was also a double garage and an RV pad located at the opposite end of the driveway.

Of course I had to have my rose gardens. And I seeded a mixture of flower seed over the septic field. Weed control was an everlasting chore but I did my best. I installed a water softener and a purification system in the utility room. We were on a local water system which drew water from the lake at the 400 foot level. This was indeed a very comfortable place to live.

In October 1992 Margaret passed away and Norman's health was failing. We went to Margaret's funeral. Now only Elsie and Norman survived in the Lyons family. That winter we had a lot of snow but we had a man with a bob-cat come as soon as it snowed and he kept our driveway clear. We closed one entrance because it was quite steep and did just fine on the other one. The road up to the complex was cleared promptly and we were never held up more than an hour or two because of the snow. In the spring a section of the main road was washed out and we had to detour a short distance but it was soon fixed.

In April of 1993 Norman passed away and we got a ride to Valleyview with Norman's son Wayne and his wife Gayle for the funeral. Wayne lives in Maple Ridge near his mom Kay. Now, at age 80, Elsie is the lone survivor of that generation.

That summer the 50th anniversary of Holland was to be celebrated. I sorely wanted to go. Elsie didn't want to go so we counted up our resources and I got the ticket on KLM for Amsterdam. Buses met us at the Airport and transported us to our host destinations. I was on a bus to Nijmegen, a city where I had spent 8 months during and after the war was over. The citizens of Holland took 8,000 veterans and 6,000 spouses into their homes for 10 days. On the way to Nijmegen a Dutch fellow sat next to me and was asking me tons of questions about the part I took in their liberation. I asked him why he was asking all those questions and he told me that he was a newspaper reporter and that it would be in the morning paper. Surely enough it was and I got a copy which I got a friend to translate for me. The bus pulled into the

Lemos barracks where I had spent most of the time in 1945. There was a young lady walking around with a card with my name on it. I introduced myself to her and her mother. They drove me to their home in a very high upper class district in Nijmegen. I was shown to a very nice room with a private bath. My host family was Will and Marianne Knoop and their daughter Benedicte. Will owned a factory where they manufactured kites. Flying kites in Europe is a very popular sport and great competitions are held throughout the land. I presented the family with some Canadian gifts including a Canadian flag. The next morning Will went out and bought a new flag pole and mounted the flag. There were Canadian flags being flown all over Holland. On a main intersection in this city there was a tulip bed and the flowers made a perfect replica of our flag. The Knoop family couldn't do enough for my comfort. Benedicte drove me anywhere I wanted to go. There were special celebrations for the Canadians every day. I went to as many as I could squeeze in. I had been corresponding with a gentleman, Philip Van Elteren, a retired University professor and a director of a Historical Society. In his research he had advertised in the Legion magazine for information on the part taken in the liberation by the Algonquin Regiment. I had responded and, as he lived in a nearby town by the name of Beek, I got Benedicte to drive me there. There was a special ceremony there dedicated to the people who had been murdered there by the Germans. As the Allies were advancing the Germans told the people to take refuge in the Synagogue. When they were all crowded in the Gestapo blew the building up and all perished. There was a Jewish lady there who had come for the celebration. She had been hidden by a Dutch family in the attic of their home and she hadn't moved from there for two years nor even dared to look out of the window.

If caught she and the Dutch family would have been slaughtered in the town square. She could speak English and I had a good conversation with her about this dreadful time.

After the ceremonies I went to the home of Philip and his wife Elizabeth. They were very charming people and he said that he may come to visit me in Canada.

Will drove me to see his Kite Factory and then to Amsterdam where I met his daughter Merribelle, a medical doctor. She was a beautiful young lady and she was looking forward to her upcoming wedding. He then took me to Marken and Vollendam. These are very popular tourist villages where the people dress in traditional Dutch clothes and run dozens of souvenir shops. I did most of my shopping here.

Will took me to the place where the paratroops were dropped in the Market Garden disaster where thousands of Allied troops died. We crossed the border to some German towns. There was no stop at the border and there was no evidence of the war since I had seen them in ruins. Back in Nijmegen we went to a special performance by the RAF band and Will introduced me to the Burgomaster, E.M. d'Hondt and I made an appointment to meet with him in his chambers set for two days later.

There was a ceremony in Nijmegen in memory for the Jewish people who were bombed by the RAF by mistake. A special monument had been erected and in place of flowers the people laid stones at the foot of the monument. I was invited to lay a stone as well. This was a very solemn ceremony at which many tears were shed.

On Sunday, May 4th there was a huge parade in Appeldoorn of all the Canadians, dressed in uniforms and 25000 people were there to give us a hero's welcome. Many broke into the parade to hug us, give us flowers, and at one point they handed out cups of beer. I don't think there has ever been such a welcome before or since. These people love Canadians and all one has to do is display a maple leaf to identify oneself and the Dutch people will pour out their appreciation for what we did for them.

We toured a battlefield near Arnhem, the site of a fierce tank battle by the fourth division. We went to the Canadian cemetery at Groesbeek where some of my comrades are buried. There was a huge ceremony there attended by Princess Margaret who was born in Ottawa where her family took refuge during the German occupation. When I got back with the Knoops I spent a quiet day with them. Marianne took me to lunch at a very exclusive estate restaurant and we ate the finest. She took me shopping and I bought gifts for the family. I woke up in the morning and heard a strange brushing noise. A servant was scrubbing down the side of the house and the gardener was trimming the shrubs. The Ditch people keep their houses scrupulously clean. There was a swimming pool in the back yard but it was a bit chilly for me. The Knoops were crazy about a tile game called Rummicub and we usually had a game before our night cap of a very fine lacquer. Marianne was a super expert at the game and taught me a few things about it. I also went to her exclusive tennis club where a fine feast was served.

A bus tour had been arranged by the president of our Algonquin Veterans' Association, Clem Beauchesne. It would take us to the point where the Regiment landed and trace the battle route through to Germany. We were taken to many spots where Algonquin's fought and died. We visited the Cemeteries and at Ardigem Cemetery I found the grave of my buddy L/Cpl. John Reinhart where I paid my respects and took pictures. We visited the Leopold Canal where I joined the Regiment on that fateful night. It looks so peaceful now and there is a street named Algonquin Stratt after the Regiment. From there we visited a few museums and at the major stops we were treated to fantastic hospitality. At Phillipine we went to a banquet and I sat next to the Mayor. She spoke perfect English and we had a very nice chat.

The next day we moved on to Isabella the scene of some very heavy fighting in the flooded areas and the dikes and polders. A monument had been erected here in honor of the Algonquin's, which Clem and I had the honor of unveiling. The school children were there and they presented each one of us with a long stem rose. I was chatting with some members of the Historical Society and I mentioned that I had been blown off the top of a tank somewhere near here. One of them spoke up and said he knew where that was. He was a young lad 10 years old and he was watching through a basement window near there and he saw the three tanks get hit. He guided the bus to the exact spot. From there we moved up to Ertvelt and on to Bergen op Zoom. This is where I had left the Regiment and went to hospital. There were quite a few of my comrades buried in the Cemetery there. We were treated to another banquet and then moved on to Nijmegen where I left the tour and went back to the Knoops.

I noticed a dark spot in the vision of my right eye and mentioned it to Benedicte. She told her mother and Marianne told me to get it attended to as soon as I could and said that it could lead to blindness

I was to catch a flight home from Amsterdam the next day but the flight was full and I had to wait two more days. The Knoop family took me to the Airport and there was a tearful farewell at the departure gate. On the trip home I had time to think about all I had seen and done and to appreciate the fine reception we had received. The plane traveled the Polar route and I was amazed to see how much of Canada was covered in snow at the end of May. I arrived home on a warm sunny day and all the spring flowers were in bloom.

Chapter Ten

I was soon back working on the landscaping at the house on Kokanee Road. There was program to clear and burn all undergrowth and low branches as a protection against forest fire. All the neighbors got together with a man from forestry to clean up the whole district of Sunset Properties, an area of about 20 acres. All deadwood had to be dragged to a safe site and burned. This was hard work but with many willing hands we had it completed in about a week.

One morning Elsie and I set out to walk the dogs. It was about a mile around the complex and we tried to do this every day. We got up to the main road and I told Elsie that I didn't feel very good and I went back to the house a phoned the doctor for an appointment. He was very busy but put me in for his last appointment. When I got to his office he took my blood pressure and asked, "How did you get here"? I told him that I drove down in the car and he said, "You are not driving it anymore today; In fact I am taking you to the hospital myself". He took me to Emergency and I was immediately admitted. There was a scurry of activity around my bed and I was told that I would not be going home. I didn't actually have a heart attack but my blood pressure was dangerously high. The next morning I was told that I would be transferred to St. Paul's hospital in Vancouver as soon as I was stabilized. A couple of days later I was loaded into an ambulance and transported to Kelowna Airport. Here they loaded me into a hospital plane and we were off. I was admitted to St. Paul's and that night I was examined by a cardiologist. He had studied my vitals and recommended immediate by-pass surgery. Some arteries in my heart were completely blocked and the operation was scheduled for the next morning. Somehow I didn't feel nervous about the operation and felt that the surgeon was the best there was. In the morning I was wheeled into surgery and that was the last thing I remember

When I came to in the recovery room my eyes saw the best sight I had ever seen. Elsie and three of my daughters were at my bedside. I was hooked up to all sorts of machines and had tubes in my mouth, nose, chest, and God knows where else. My eyes closed and I was out of it until the next day. The first few days are rather vague and there was quite a bit of pain. The staff there was fantastic and treated me with the best of care. I was transferred to a ward with three other guys on the third day. We were all in there for similar reasons and were soon telling jokes and having a great time considering the state we were in. I was discharged on the sixth day and Elsie was there to drive me home in the car.

Before all this happened I had see an eye specialist and he told me that I had macular degeneration in my right eye and would get me an appointment in Vancouver as soon as possible. There was a 3 month waiting list. About a month after my heart operation I went to the General Hospital in Vancouver. I had a torn retina and Dr. Ma attempted to repair it but it didn't work. Finally the whole retina fell into the bottom of the eye ball. After three trips to Vancouver Dr. Ma told me that the best thing would be to remove that eye and explained how I would be fitted with a prosthesis to which I consented. The surgery was so expertly done that the eye sack and muscle are coordinated with the left eye that people don't know that I have only one eye. I was fitted with a lens that matches the left eye perfectly. It is definitely a handicap but I manage OK. I drove the car for a few years but have had to give it two years ago.

We lived up at Judy's house for the five years but were finding it a bit too much driving back and forth; sometimes three times in a day. We bought another house in town across the street from the one we lived in on 21st Avenue. We knew the house and the owner and got a good deal on it. Here we were into renovation again. It was good house but needed upgrading. We spent two years getting it into shape. I did a lot of the work but hired tradesmen for most of it

We lived in that house for five years but found the stairs to be a bit too much and decided to hunt for a level entrance. We looked at many options and one day our real estate agent told us that perhaps we should up the price we were willing to pay. He showed us to a couple more houses and finally a duplex in Gracelands. It is a senior's complex and as soon as we walked through it we were both highly impressed and it didn't take very long to place an offer on it. All was accepted and we moved in. All the outside work is done for us and we look after the inside. However we have enlarged the concrete patio at the back and built a ramp from the kitchen to the patio. We also had grab bars installed in the bathrooms and installed a second stair rail to the basement.

In the year 2007 Elsie had a stroke and was in hospital for three months. I had to take over the housekeeping chores and help Elsie dress. She gradually improved but is still left with very limited use of her let hand. To add to this, in 2008,

Elsie fell and broke her hip and once again was laid up in hospital...After a bit of a wait she got a hip replacement and quite quickly recovered from that. We realized that we were going to need some long-term care. Donna was not very happy with her job in Niagara Falls and we offered her a job as our care giver. She came to live with us and literally took over. She does the housework and the grocery shopping and all of the other household chores. She makes delicious meals and drives us where we have to go. Both Elsie and I had given up driving the car and Donna took over the driving.

In August of 2008 I was sitting in my chair and got a strange feeling in my chest. I asked Donna to drive me to the hospital. I was admitted right away and was told that it was a heart attack and a very good thing that I got there promptly. After I was stabilized I was scheduled for a trip to St. Paul's hospital in Vancouver for an angioplasty procedure in which two stents were implanted. I was only there for two days and then back home and feeling much better. As the summer passed I was not able to do very much without getting out of breath.

This condition worsened and by March of 2009 I was not able to walk more than half a block without having to stop and rest for a few minutes. The Ice Capades were coming to Vernon and we got tickets for the three of us. On the evening of the show I was not feeling very well but went to the show. I saw the first part of the show and then I knew that I had to go to the hospital and called for an ambulance. They took me to emergency and I was admitted immediately. The doctor told me that I had another heart attack and would have to go to Vancouver for surgery. A few days later I was flown to Vancouver by air ambulance and admitted to St. Paul's hospital. I had another angioplasty procedure and a stent was inserted into a main artery. I was there for a few days and then flown back to Vernon by air ambulance and ad mitted to Vernon Jubilee hospital. I am home now and feel better than I have for a long time.

Now I can get back to my writing and complete this book and also my new book, "Outer Space and Beyond". I can now get both books off to the publisher and they will soon be on the shelves of the book stores.

I close this story of my life with the satisfaction that I have had a long and very fruitful life. At the age of 84 I look with satisfaction that all of my children have done very well; all with professional jobs. Elsie and I have 12 grandchildren and 17 great grandchildren. At my age I don't pretend to know all their names but I love to see them when they come to visit. We intend to stay here as long as we can and stay as comfortable as we can.

THE END